MED SCHOOL
after
MENOPAUSE
The Journey of my Soul

ANN CHARLOTTE VALENTIN
N.M.D.

Divine Publishing
Phoenix, Arizona, U.S.A.

Divine Publishing is a division of Divine Spiritual Essence.
www.DivineSpiritualEssence.com

Text design and layout by Sarah Flood-Baumann.

To send correspondence to the author of this book,
please visit www.DrLotte.com

Visit www.DrLotte.com and enter the code below to receive a free meditation.

Code: **Bookpromo**

ACKNOWLEDGEMENTS

Many people have touched my life in different ways to help me become the person I am today. It takes a village to heal, and it takes a village to bring out the best in people. We come into this life with many people and animals to help us along our path. We just have to pause for a moment to realize who they are. The list below are people who have made significant contributions to my life in one way or another, but if you are not mentioned and you have impacted my life, know that you are special, too, and it was simply an oversight on my part!

Alanna for always being there and providing endless spiritual and emotional support through my life journey; without her birth, I would never have become who I am today.

Kim, my soul sister, and her husband, Mark, for always providing support and trusting in my path.

Jesse, Oliver, and Nicole for always inspiring me by what they do.

John for always providing support and trusting in my abilities and pushing me to go to medical school when I was ready to back out.

Aaron for his many interpretations on spirituality and life.

Shelly for always being there in my time of need.

Monica for being my friend since birth and always believing in me.

Kristin for bringing through the message from the spirit world that I needed to go to Arthur Findlay College in England to develop as a medium.

My teachers at Arthur Findlay College—Mia, Eileen, Bill, and Angie—for helping me develop into a medium and trusting in my path.

Shaman Itzak Beery for teaching me to trust my soul's purpose.

My teachers in medical school who taught me how to become a doctor.

To all my family and extended family for always supporting me in life.

A special thank you also goes to my editor, Amanda Horan, for providing tireless editing and guidance as well as Katrina Robinson for her excellent proofreading.

Thank you to my dog, Priyala, and cats, Bodhi and Samadhi, for keeping me grounded on a daily basis.

Thank you to all my family, friends, and pets in the spirit world for the support you gave me during your life and your continuous guidance you provide each day.

Thank you to everyone else I have failed to mention.

I love you all!
Dr. Lotte Valentin

CONTENTS

1

A BRUSH WITH DEATH

The Earthquake

It was 1:30 a.m. on June 28, 1992. I experienced a strong contraction and knew right away I was in labor. My body tingled
with excitement as I realized my third child was ready to arrive
into the world. As my parents were visiting from Sweden to
help care for our two boys, ages six and three and a half, my
husband and I took off for the hospital in Anaheim, California.

During the ride, I experienced another strong contraction, and
as my second child had been born during my fifth contraction, I
worried the baby would be born in the car. I felt very apprehensive
and worried we wouldn't make it in time. My palms were sweaty,
and I could feel my heart pounding in my chest. I told my husband to step on the gas and drive as quickly as he could. I kept
focusing on remaining calm and breathing slowly, as I feared my
anxiety would bring on the birth. As we arrived at the hospital, I
thought I was safe and took a deep breath of relief. I was quickly
transferred into a wheelchair and taken to a birthing room.

The room was modern and quite large, with huge wall-to-wall
darkened glass windows. The contractions kept getting stronger,
and I was already feeling tired from the continuous cramping.

At 4:57 a.m., my contractions were three minutes apart when
suddenly, I felt the earth starting to shake beneath me. I knew
right away it was going to be a big earthquake. I felt scared

as the hospital started to shake more and more violently. My body was entering the fight-or-flight response. I felt like a dog with its tail between its legs, frozen in fear. I could feel the adrenalin rushing through my veins, but I wasn't able to move or take shelter and felt trapped, powerless, and vulnerable on the table. I had no protection from the impending disaster as I lay exposed half-naked on the table like a beached whale with my large belly. I was filled with fear, and my chest felt tight and constricted. My breathing became shallow, and my brain felt like it was moving in slow motion. It was as if I were standing at death's door about to be swallowed up by the earth itself. I could feel the hands and arms of my husband and the nurses clinging to my body and bed, holding on for their life.

The 7.3 earthquake was now in full force, and the hospital, which was in the eastern part of Anaheim, California, and fairly close to the epicenter of the quake, was now rolling from side to side. As this was a newer hospital, it was built on rollers to withstand earthquakes better. It was as if I were on board a ship in the ocean in the middle of a storm making it very difficult to keep my balance standing up. All the medical instruments banged on the metal trays as the shaking continued. The midwives and my husband leaned over me on the birthing table in order not to fall as well as making sure I wouldn't fly off the bed. At this point, it was the second time in my life when I thought I was going to die.

My mind, now in a state of panic, thought, *I didn't think my life was going to end this way. I feel so bad for my boys if they have to grow up without parents and my unborn child that may never be born.* I felt my life flashing before my eyes as I wondered if we would survive. I worried about the building collapsing or the large windows or ceiling tiles crashing down on us, burying us in rubble. After what seemed like an eternity the shaking finally stopped and we had lost all power in the hospital. Everything was eerily calm and quiet. I instantly expressed gratitude to God for being alive, even though I wasn't sure if there was a God or higher power of divinity. It was something that just came out of me naturally from gratitude of being unharmed. After all, we had survived, and none of us were injured.

I worried about the patients in the hospital that were on life support and wondered if they were okay. I sighed in relief as the generators kicked in and we had the light equivalent of a night light in the birthing room. My labor had stopped due to the intense fear I had experienced during the shaking. When a mother is in the birthing process and experiencing great fear, the body doesn't have time for birthing, and labor can stop temporarily. This is exactly what had happened to my body.

After my husband got word from my parents that they and our two young boys were okay, I relaxed, and my contractions started back up again.

At 6:20 a.m., my daughter was born. I was so excited about her birth and couldn't wait to hold her. We waited for the next contraction to deliver the placenta, but there was no contraction. The nurses and midwives exchanged nervous looks with one another. We waited and waited, growing more concerned as time passed. Finally, I experienced a contraction, and it felt as if someone had ripped off a piece of duct tape from the inside of my uterus. I told the midwife what I had experienced and asked her to please check the placenta to see if there was a piece missing. She held up the placenta, flipped it from one side to the other, and stated it looked whole. With the dim lighting in the birthing room, it wasn't easy to see if only a small piece the size of your pinky nail was missing from the placenta, which could then cause an infection in the uterus afterward. I was relieved it seemed the placenta was whole and stopped worrying.

The phlebotomist entered the room to collect a post-delivery blood sample from me. As he was in the process of inserting the needle into my arm, a second earthquake struck. His eyes, fixated and enlarged, stared straight into mine. He looked like he was in a state of panic. At first, I was worried this earthquake was going to be bigger than the one we had just experienced, but as it continued, I realized it was of a slightly lesser magnitude. We assured him this was a smaller earthquake than the first one and to not be alarmed, even though the hospital was again violently shaking and rolling from side to side. With these affirmations, he relaxed and became calmer. As he had been at home, farther away from the epicenter when the first quake hit, he thought this earthquake was of a larger magnitude than the first one. There were two people killed and over a hundred people injured during the Landers quake, and we were all thankful we were safe and unharmed. It was the largest quake to hit California in forty years and is one of the seven largest quakes ever, even bigger than the famous Northridge quake. The reason there wasn't more damage was that the epicenter was in the desert.

The nurses cleaned up my baby girl and gave her to me so I could hold and bond with her. I was so excited to finally be holding my newborn baby—my heart was filled with love and gratitude.

As I kissed my baby's head while she began to nurse, I felt excruciating pain and arched backward, yelling to the nurses and my husband to take my daughter. The pain was so sudden and severe I was unable to hold her. I was transferred to another bed in the birthing room where two midwives massaged my uterus, which was very painful, causing several large blood clots to appear between my legs on the table. I was exhausted from giving birth and experiencing so much trauma at the same time. I just wanted it to be over so I could go home. After several minutes of massage, the blood clots seemed to subside and I was put on a Pitocin IV drip to contract the uterus to stop the bleeding. As my condition stabilized, I was transferred to a floor higher up in the hospital.

As I was lying in the bed, the aftershocks continued to shake through the hospital on and off for the rest of my stay. The news station was on TV and kept reporting all the aftershocks as they happened throughout the area. I worried there would be another quake, maybe larger than the first one. If that would happen, would I survive? It seemed the last twenty-four hours had consisted of being in a constant survival mode. The earth-shaking seemed much worse at the higher hospital floor I was now on, but I counted my blessings that I was unharmed from the earthquake and that my uterus was on the mend, or so I thought.

My mind wandered to my sister-in-law, who was fighting for her life, battling cancer in her mid-forties. I was wondering if she would survive. Life all of a sudden seemed more fragile than ever before. I realized that life could really be taken away from you in a split second. The non-stop contractions from the IV drip and the aftershocks from the earthquake had made me exhausted. I was relieved to finally be released after my forty-eight-hour stay and was looking forward to going home. What I didn't know was that my ordeal was far from over.

A Brush with Death

As each day passed, I kept experiencing pain in my vaginal area as if someone were pressing down on it from the inside of my body. The pain was so bad at times it would force me to sit down. If I were in a store, I would have to sit on the floor or the bottom shelf in order to relieve the pain. I thought it must be due to my baby having been so large, weighing 9.2 pounds, and that it was just my vaginal tissue healing. Little did I know or understand what was really going on.

On Wednesday, July 8, my friends were holding a baby shower in the park for me and I put the baby and the two boys in the car while my parents stayed at the house. As I arrived at the park, I felt as though I needed to go change my menstrual pad and headed to the park bathroom. While on the toilet, a blood clot the size of a baby's head emerged from me, and as I stared at this enormous blood clot in the toilet, I immediately knew something was terribly wrong. I felt scared, nauseous, and weak just looking at it. It was as if I had a big empty ice-cold hole in my stomach. It took all my power to remain calm so I would not vomit from pure fear.

As my children had accompanied me to the bathroom, I tried to not look worried, as I didn't want them to be scared. I went back, told my friend what had happened, quickly put the boys and baby back in the car, and drove back home, just a few blocks from the park. I kept myself calm, though I felt nauseous with fear, as my children kept asking why we were leaving the park. I told them I wasn't feeling well and we needed to get back home to grandma and grandpa. As I drove, my mind desperately tried to make sense of what was happening, and it all seemed surreal. I was petrified I would start bleeding again and maybe pass out before reaching our house and getting the children home safely. As I entered our house and lay down on the bed, I told my parents what had happened. I was relieved to be back home but felt shaky, dizzy, and weak and was very concerned about the size of the blood clot and what might be wrong with me My parents called my husband, who came home from work and took me to the emergency room.

As we arrived at the ER, I explained to the doctor what had happened. They performed a manual examination of my vagina and uterus and told me not much bleeding was going on anymore. They kept me for observation for a few hours. The doctor in the ER thought the hemorrhaging could have been caused by the shedding of a second uterine lining and I was released from the hospital without any further workup.

In the evening of the next day, Thursday, July 9, I went to the bathroom thinking I needed to urinate. Another enormous blood clot the size of a baby's head appeared. Again, I stared into the toilet at the large blood clot knowing something was terribly wrong. My husband called the hospital and asked if we should come back to the ER. We weren't sure what to do considering the ER hadn't done anything to stop the bleeding the day before. As he was on the phone, my bleeding stopped and it was decided I should see the doctor in the morning at 10:00 a.m. in Huntington Beach, California, where we lived at the time.

The next day, Friday, July 10, I saw the OBGYN doctor, who examined me and made the same statement as the hospital staff had two days earlier, that there was not much bleeding going on right now and sometimes there can be two uterine linings being shed after birth. No other exams or blood work was done, and I was sent on my way.

That evening, another large blood clot appeared when using the restroom, and I again stared into the toilet knowing something was terribly wrong. This time, we decided to go back to the emergency room, as we didn't know what else to do.

Upon arriving, I told the doctor how I had been hemorrhaging every day for the past three days and I was again put in a room for observation. I was glad to be back in the ER, as it felt safer than being at home. A doctor and his assistant entered the room to examine me and determined nothing much was happening at the moment, as there was only a trickle of blood visible during the exam. They left me in the room, and I was to be held for observation.

While I was lying on the bed in the ER, I finally started bleeding again. I remember feeling very happy about it, as I figured they were finally going to figure out something was actually wrong with me. As I was lying there in a pool of my own blood with the door shut and no bell to ring for help, a nurse finally came in to check on me. As she opened the door, her jaw dropped as she realized how much I had been bleeding. The panic that was written all over her face made me understand she knew something was terribly wrong. She quickly alerted the other doctors and nurses for help. I could hear the STAT call in the hospital loudspeakers as the call for "OBGYN STAT TO THE ER" echoed throughout the hallway! Within a minute, an out-of-breath middle-aged doctor ran into my room followed by a younger doctor. I remember feeling relieved they had finally sent a doctor who looked like he had been through a few things in his profession and that he most likely would know what to do with me. This was the doctor that saved my life. I don't even know his name, but I'm very thankful for his quick and correct actions, as without him, I would most certainly not be alive today.

The doctor looked in the wastebasket where they had stuffed my bloody papers and asked how much I had been bleeding. I quickly told him that this was the third day I'd been hemorrhaging, so he and his assistant examined me to see how much bleeding was going on at the moment. As they examined me, another large blood clot surfaced, and I tried to sit up to tell him I wasn't feeling well. He quickly pushed me back down on the bed and started tipping it backward to lower my head in order to keep the blood in the heart and vital organs.

As this was taking place, the room quickly filled with hospital staff and I could hear them all talking and firing instructions of what to do next. I started to feel very weak, and I was glad I was in the ER and not at home. There was a nurse on my left side trying to place an IV in my arm, and on my right side there was a nurse who put a blood pressure cuff on my arm. I felt weaker and weaker, like I was falling. It was as if I had jumped out of an airplane without a parachute and was rapidly falling toward the ground. I was mustering up every ounce I had within me to hold on to my life. Life, something I had been taking for granted, was suddenly barely within reach. The nurse on my right was quoting my blood pressure and yelled out in a panicked voice, "FIFTY OVER FIFTEEN! HURRY." My senses all of a sudden seemed superhuman, and my hearing was so clear it was as if I were wearing some supernatural headphones. It was shortly after this moment that I realized I was dying. The *knowing* that I was dying was a very different feeling from *thinking* I may die. As I was dying, I *knew* I was dying; there was no thinking, *Oh my God, I'm going to die!* I was now in a complete state of sheer panic. There was a realization of the fact that *I was dying*! I felt myself getting weaker and weaker. I tried to hold on to my life with all my power. I felt like I was hanging off a cliff in the Grand Canyon using only my nails and could fall to my death at any second. Even though I was an atheist at the time, I instinctively prayed to God to save my life. *I have three children under the age of six! They need a mother! Please let me live!* I pleaded with God. I felt like I was falling, just rapidly falling in space. I struggled to hold on and stay inside my body.

The pull on my soul was too great, and I found myself floating out of my body. All of a sudden, I was hovering about two to three feet above myself. There was an instantaneous feeling of unconditional love and peace. A knowing that all of life was very divine. Everything made perfect sense on "the other side," as if I had knowledge of all that was when outside my body. There was an understanding that I had access to all information—past, present, and future—all at the same time. There was no time in the state I was in. I was in some kind of in-between state, not on earth and not in heaven. I felt as though there were a piece of me still in my body. I was somehow attached to my body even though I was hovering in space. There was a sense of an energetic attachment to my body as if my soul had just stepped outside its house temporarily but still knew it lived in there. The first thing I noticed was that I was still alive. I was still there, just outside my body! *How can this be?* I thought. *How can I still be alive but without my body? How can I think and process what is happening without my body?*

All of a sudden, I was sucked back into my body, like a giant vacuum hose, similar to how Tim Allen in the movie *The Santa Clause* goes through the chimney to deliver Christmas presents. I could feel the IV fluids rushing through my veins, like a cartoon figure undergoing surgery. Everybody in the room was clapping and cheering as I regained consciousness, like a hospital TV show.

I felt relieved I was back in my body. I had made it! I had survived! The lead doctor looked quite pale and alarmed, as I'm sure he was catching his breath after my close call with death. I tried to move my head slightly to look at him, and he yelled at me, "DON'T MOVE," as the situation was still most likely very fragile and they were afraid of losing me again. At this point, I was injected with various medications to stop the bleeding, and the doctor said he needed to give me a blood transfusion. I told him I didn't want a blood transfusion, and he asked if I had a religious belief that prevented me from accepting a transfusion. As this was 1992, there was a lot of news in the press about people who had received blood transfusions and then later been diagnosed with AIDS. I told him I had three children under the age of six and didn't want to learn in five to six years that I had contracted AIDS. The doctor nodded, and the look on his face told me he understood exactly what I meant. He promised to see what he could do to avoid the transfusion.

My body started to shake violently due to being cold, and they covered me with several warm blankets. My father and husband entered the room to say goodbye before returning home. The look on my father's face as he kissed my forehead to say goodbye was of great concern. That look of pain on his face, it told me how much he loved me and that he understood how serious the condition was and how close he had been to losing his daughter. What I had just experienced was very confusing for me at this time in my life, as I didn't believe the soul survived the death of the body.

This poem that I wrote in 2003, which was eleven years after my brush with death and what is called a near-death experience or NDE, describes my experience. The eleventh year is the year I really processed what had happened to me; therefore, a lot of writing and reading took place that year. The poem is called "Thank You, God," but it could as well be called "Thank You, Divine Source."

"Thank You, God"

I lie on the table in the emergency room.
A t-shirt and a sheet of paper is covering my naked body.
I'm tan.
It's summer.
I look like the picture of health.
My body feels tired.

I'm by myself now.
I feel deserted.
It's getting late.
I think of my husband and father in the waiting area.
Waiting, holding my baby.
I think of my caring mother at home,
attending to my two young boys.

I've hemorrhaged three times in three days.
I know something is wrong.
A doctor and his assistant enter.
He examines me.
Nothing is happening now.
They leave.
I wait.

My mind is wandering.
I think of my ten-day-old infant.
I'm wondering if she's hungry.
My breasts fill with milk at the thought.
My breasts begin to spray a fine mist of milk.
My t-shirt gets soaked.
I can hear the doctors and nurses laughing and talking.
They must be on a break.

I feel a large blood clot slip out through my vagina.
The size of my husband's large, strong fists.
It feels like I'm giving birth to a large bowl of JELL-O.
I feel relieved I'm bleeding again.
I feel elated someone might realize there is something wrong
with me.
I don't want to wait any longer.
I don't want them to tell me once again they can see no wrong.

A nurse opens the door to check on me.
I see the look of panic on her face.
She stares at the pool of blood between my legs.
She sticks her head out the door.
She yells for a doctor.
She quickly cleans up my mess.
She throws the bloody paper away.
She puts down new, clean paper.
I hear the page for a doctor on the hospital loudspeaker.
"STAT to the emergency room!"
I feel content and optimistic.
They've discovered something is wrong with me.
I know I'm on my way to get well.

The doctor arrives.
He looks straight into my eyes.
He looks at the bloody paper in the wastebasket.
His face is serious and worried.
He asks how long I've been bleeding.
An assistant enters the room.
The doctor examines me.
I pass another large blood clot.
This one, larger than the others.
Bigger than my husband's fist.

I try to sit up.
I tell the doctor I'm not feeling well.
I start to fade.
The doctor and his assistant jump to their feet.
The door opens.
The room quickly fills with people dressed in white and green.
My table surrounded.

I hear the noises of the doctors and nurses working.
Working to save my life.
I feel the table being tipped.
I feel my head getting lower and lower.
I feel my feet pointing toward the ceiling.
I feel the hands of the nurse working on my arm.
I feel the needle trying to enter my vein.
I'm thinking, *What's taking them so long?*
I feel the blood pressure cuff tightening around my arm.
I can hear the nurse on my right quoting my blood pressure.
The sound of her voice, it is so clear.
That voice, forever imprinted in my brain's auditory memory.
So clear, clearer than anything else I've ever heard,
as clear as a pair of supersonic headphones of the future not
yet discovered.
It is in this clear voice,
I hear the panic in her voice
as she quotes my falling blood pressure.
"Fifty over fifteen, hurry," she yells out.
I can feel my body getting weaker and weaker.
I can feel my blood pressure plummet.
I feel like I'm riding an elevator that has lost its cables.
Dropping by the force of gravity alone.
Plunging toward the bottom of its shaft.
Falling toward its final destination.
I realize I'm dying.

My mind quickly tries to hold on to life.
It tries to reason.
It asks, *How can this be?*
It says, *I have three young children and a husband.*
It tries to hold on to reality.
It says, *I can't die!*
My then-scientific, atheist personality instinctively does
what it knows it has to do.
My Body
My Spirit
My Soul
It Prays
It prays to God to save my life.

I float out of my body.
I enter a stage of definite relaxation.
It is so peaceful, tranquil, harmonious.
Words, insufficient to accurately describe the moment.
Everything seems so serene.
It feels so colossal.
Euphoric
Bliss
Unconditional Love and Peace

I'm still me!
It's me.
My spirit.
My soul.
Me!

Impromptu, I get sucked back into my body.
Like a giant vacuum cleaner.
Stronger than life itself.
I travel faster than the speed of sound.
Faster than the speed of light.
It is instantaneous.
It happens hypersonically.
It is hard for my earthly brain to comprehend.
I feel like I've been let in on a secret of life.
A secret of life the human race is not supposed to know.

I feel the fluids from the IV rush through my veins.
Like a cartoon figure undergoing surgery.
I feel the fluids go up through my arm.
I feel it travel through my veins into my heart.
I feel it travel down through the veins in my legs.
I hear the doctors and nurses applaud and cheer.
I feel relieved.
I feel exuberant.
I feel blessed.
I thank God for saving my life.

Thank you, God.

ACV

After they had covered me in warm blankets, I was transferred
from the ER to another floor in the hospital and was kept over-
night. The automatic blood pressure cuff was tightening around
my arm what seemed like every five minutes. There was a long
ribbon of paper from the machine on to the floor that recorded
all the blood pressure readings. My head pounded, and I felt

very cold from not having enough blood in my body.

As I lay in the hospital room, I was aware of my sister-in-law, who had just passed three days earlier on July 7. I felt as though she was in the left corner of the ceiling looking down on me. There seemed to be some telepathic communication between us.

"You will be okay," she told me.

I wondered if I was going crazy. *How can I hear her?* I thought. Was I really communicating with her? I wasn't sure what to believe, as I didn't have a scientific explanation for it. I didn't share this with anyone, as I thought my family would think I must have been hallucinating, and I was worried how they would react if I told them. If we all shared our paranormal experiences with one another, they probably wouldn't be as unusual as we think they are.

The next morning, there was a team of physicians and nurses making the patient rounds. The lead physicians ordered his staff to "ambulate" me. They pushed the button on my bed to raise me up to a sitting position. My head and upper body were slowly raised. As the bed was slowly rising, I experienced the most excruciating pain in my head. It was as if someone had taken a sword and cut my head in half. I couldn't speak or moan. On a scale of one to ten, the pain was a ten and the worst pain I've ever experienced. Even worse than giving birth with a dislocated disc like I had done with my first child. They helped me stand, and with the help of a nurse, I walked to the doorway, at which point everything started to fade and I told them I felt like I was going to faint. They quickly found a wheelchair and put me back in bed; I was to stay in the hospital another twenty-four hours.

The next morning, a nice nurse came to my room to give me instructions for my discharge. I managed to sit up on the bed by slowly raising myself, letting my head and body adjust gradually. My head was still pounding as if a bowling ball was being swung from side to side inside my head. I was told my body was making new red blood cells quickly and even though I probably wouldn't feel very well for a couple of weeks due to being so anemic, I would most likely recover quickly as I was otherwise young and healthy.

The nurse asked me if I had experienced anything unusual in the ER when I was hemorrhaging. Even though she seemed very nice, I was afraid to tell anyone in the hospital about my experience of leaving my body, as I thought they would think I was crazy and either put me in the psychiatric inpatient ward or medicate me. After all, I wasn't able to make sense of my experience, so I didn't think the hospital staff would be able to either. I was happy to return back home knowing the problem was now solved and I was on the road to recovery, or so I thought.

Weak

I don't have many memories from the weeks that followed and have been told I mostly slept as my parents cared for our two young boys and baby infant girl. I remember my mother and the boys waking me up to bring me food and my mother feeding me spinach omelets to help my body produce iron and red blood cells. It was now mid-July in Huntington Beach, California, and I was lying in bed with two wool blankets covering my body and my ice-cold hands and feet. I could hear my children playing in the wading pool in the backyard, and I wished I were outside with them. My head was resting directly on the mattress, as the incline of the pillow made me feel faint and caused my head to pound and hurt even more. I was so weak. I could barely stay awake. This poem sums up my state at the time.

"Weak"

Someone calls on the phone.
I lie in my bed.
I say hello.
I fall asleep while they are talking.
I apologize.
I hang up.
I'm too weak to talk.
Someone visits.
A dear friend.
I slowly rise.
My head is pounding.
The pain is excruciating.
I slowly make my way down the hallway.
I start to faint.
I throw myself on the sofa.
I raise my legs up.
I feel the blood reach my pounding head.
I sip some tea lying down.
I listen to my friend talk.
I fall asleep.
I'm too weak to listen.

Someone is talking in the kitchen.
I hear the voices of my parents and husband.
I hear the voices of my two young boys.
I hear them talking and laughing.
I lie in my bed.
I feel cold.
I feel hungry.
I feel weak.

I wish I had the strength to join them.
I wish I had the strength to shout out for them to come.
I wish I was well.
I wait.
I fall asleep.
I'm too weak.

Someone opens the door.
I hear the high-pitched voices of my boys.
"She's awake," they say in unison.
The boys are happy.
Their mom is awake.
I see my mother coming down the hallway.
Two towheaded boys following closely behind.
Like a parade they enter my room.
My mother, carrying a tray of food.
The boys, carrying drinks and snacks for themselves.
The food, it smells so good.
I eat.
We talk.
We laugh.
I thank them for the food.
I go back to sleep.
I'm too weak.

ACV, November 2003

I was told later that my parents changed their return tickets back
to Sweden twice, and when they finally returned back home
sometime in August, my mother-in-law came from Florida to
take over the care. It wasn't until sometime in September that
I was finally strong enough to sit up. When it was time for my

mother-in-law to return to Florida, she hired cleaning help to reduce the burden on us, as I was unable to carry out those tasks yet. I was still very weak, and I wasn't able to stand up for very long or walk through the house without feeling dizzy and faint. I had never felt so helpless in my entire life. It was a roller-coaster of emotions from being angry I had experienced so many traumatic events, to being grateful to be alive. I was stuck with my current physical condition, and there wasn't anything I could do to speed up my healing process. I had to be patient and let everything run its course. I knew I wasn't going to just wake up and feel great the next day. It was a slow process of moving toward wellness, and as each day passed, I would be grateful for still being alive and for my children having a mother. What I didn't know at the time was what the outcome of this experience would lead to and what else was coming my way.

MESSAGE | Live each day as if it is your last.

Exercise: Remind yourself how precious life is and that anything can happen to you at any given time that may change your life forever. Take the opportunities to enjoy your life whenever you can. This can be something as simple as going to the movies with a friend or enjoying a nice dinner. Keep a daily log and write down each day one or more events or things you did that made the day special. Did you give a nice compliment to someone, or did someone give you a compliment that changed your day? Did you help an elderly person crossing the street or hold the door open for someone who returned your favor with a smile? Small acts of kindness can change both your and the recipient's lives. Find something you can enjoy each day to bring love and gratitude for your life to the present moment.

2

THE ROCKING CHAIR

Life Is a Gift
A few months had passed since my daughter's birth, and I was still feeling very weak. I was forced to sit down most of the time, and I spent the next six to nine months sitting in the black rocking chair. I was too weak to stand up long enough to make lunch for the boys. It was an awful feeling not being able to carry out even simple tasks without feeling absolutely exhausted. I wondered if this was how old people felt, incapable and lonely. I felt bad I hadn't made a bigger effort to help my grandmother when she was alive. I felt so helpless and hopeless to have to rely on others for help with the simplest tasks like doing dishes and laundry. I could imagine how old people felt and how they might be too embarrassed to ask for help or not want to bother their children and loved ones. It made me more aware to always offer help to others in need. I felt like the healing process was taking forever—much longer than I had anticipated. I wanted to feel normal again so I could take my children to the playground and see my friends.

Day in and day out, I sat in the rocking chair, praying to stay alive while holding and rocking my infant girl in my arms. I would visualize myself running on the beach playing with the children. I could hear the boys' laughter from their room as they were playing. I now realize it was my maternal instinct and the power of the Divine Feminine that kept me alive. The record *Watermark* by Enya played non-stop, as I was too weak to stand up and change the record. As I'm writing this, I found the album on iTunes and am now playing it for the first time in twenty years. After I healed, I threw the record away, as I didn't want to be reminded of the past. I always focused on the current moment and moving forward. As I hear the first song on the album *Watermark*, I'm flooded with emotions of both gratitude and pain. I'm thankful for the music, which helped me heal, but am also reminded of the health crisis I was going through at that time. What I hadn't grieved then, I had to grieve now. It's all a process. What you don't process in the moment, you will have to process at a later time.

Every night when I went to bed, I would pray that I would wake up the next morning. I said this prayer each night before I went to sleep: *Please let me wake up tomorrow; my children need me.* There were days when I felt so weak and sick, I wished I would die. My own thoughts scared me. I would immediately switch my thought pattern and visualize myself as healthy. I kept focusing on gratitude, the present moment, and anything positive I could think of. I wouldn't allow myself to have any negative thoughts.

One night when I said my prayer to please let me wake up the next day, I heard a voice. The voice didn't come from inside my head, nor did it come externally from using my ears. It came from somewhere else, outside of me but not through my ears. It was present everywhere and not like a thought or hearing music inside your head. The voice said: "You will be okay." The message was so clear, as if someone had reached through the veil from the other side and touched my soul. There was something divine about the message. Instantaneously, I knew the message to be true. I lived by this message. I trusted it instinctively. There was no more doubt if I would heal. I now knew I would heal. Life often brings us different types of struggles that may be physical, emotional, or spiritual. As hard as life can seem during these times, never forget that life is a divine gift allowing our souls to grow. Don't ever give up hope!

Gratitude

Three months had passed after my brush with death, and my husband had taken a new job. We were on the ninety-day wait period to receive new medical insurance. Paying COBRA to keep our current insurance for the entire family was too expensive, and as I had lost faith in the medical system after what I had experienced, we decided to go without insurance for three months. However, we had no idea what was coming our way.

I started walking one house to the left and one house to the right of our house in order to try to build up my muscles and stamina. This little walk was absolutely exhausting, and I would have to go inside and rest after five to ten minutes of walking. I was still feeling very weak and experienced dizziness when standing up for more than five minutes but figured I would gain strength slowly by increasing exercise.

The fall came and went, and I slowly kept getting stronger and stronger. By December, six months after my daughter was born, I wanted to prove to myself that I was strong enough to put the kids in the car and drive two blocks to the grocery store to purchase milk and ice cream. Off we went!

The boys were very excited about the outing and their mom getting stronger. They were singing and jumping up and down from sheer joy at the mere thought of getting ice cream. I was equally excited about the outing. It was so rewarding to be able to walk into the grocery store, and I felt like I was finally on the mend. We retrieved the milk and ice cream and headed to the checkout. As we stood in line to check out, I started to feel weak and dizzy. I worried I had taken on too much too quickly. I now realized it wasn't the greatest idea to take the kids to the store—what if I passed out? I had felt so much stronger at home, but the short walk from the car and in the store had made me feel weak and dizzy again. I quickly paid and managed to get us all back to the car safely.

I was now as excited as the boys were about their ice cream, as I had proved to myself I was getting stronger and capable of a short errand despite the dizzy feeling. I never imagined that being able to go to the grocery store could create so much gratitude. I was again reminded to never take my health and life for granted. Be grateful for all that you can do each day.

Christmas

Christmas came and went, and we didn't have a lot of money, as we were living on one income, which was supporting all five of us. We couldn't afford many extras, and we had a small ham and a can of cranberries with potatoes for Christmas dinner. This was much less than we had ever had before, but we were thankful we could afford food at all. If our parents had known, I'm sure they would have gladly helped us financially. However, we were too stoic to ask for help at the time. We knew our own parents had struggled much more than us when they were young, and we felt blessed we were better off financially than they had been during the WWII era. When my parents were young and my father was in medical school, he would cycle to school even when the temperature was forty below and his glasses would freeze to his temples. They couldn't afford to put anything on their bread except for butter. In comparison, we knew we should be happy with what we had. We were again reminded to count our blessings. The boys received a few five-dollar gifts of Ninja

Turtles, as that was what they really wished for and all we could afford. We had both grown up experiencing abundance during the holiday season, so this felt sparse to me. However, this taught me that the holiday isn't about money or presents. Holidays, just as life itself, is about sharing your love with others. Why had our past Christmas holidays turned into consumerism? Why had we lost track of who we truly were as human beings? We sat around the Christmas tree watching the boys play with their new toys and were grateful for me being alive, my husband getting better jobs, and things overall going in the right direction.

Another Problem Surfaces

We were just about to receive medical insurance, as we had almost completed the ninety-day wait period, when my husband received a job offer with a higher income. He asked me for advice, and I encouraged him to accept the job offer. It was now the end of January of 1993 and we all came down with the flu except for the baby. As we didn't have medical insurance, we went to a walk-in clinic and I was told I was very congested with bronchitis and that there was blood and pus in my ear from a raging ear infection, which had caused me to also lose my hearing in this ear. My husband had a diagnosis of pneumonia, as did the boys. I was exhausted trying to care for the boys and myself, and was relieved when we were all given antibiotics. After taking the medicine for seven days, everyone in the family was on the mend—except for me. My chest congestion kept getting worse, and it was difficult to breathe, and I decided I needed to return to the walk-in clinic. The doctors were surprised to see me again and took a blood sample. When they returned to the room, they asked if I had leukemia or AIDS. I told them the story of how I had been hemorrhaging after birth and was then injected with antibiotics and other medications.

After they injected me with the antibiotics, they realized they had injected me with a medication that I was possibly allergic to. They kept me for observation for two hours to make sure I wasn't going to have any symptoms. While I was lying on the table in the exam room for observation, I said this prayer: *Dear God, if you allowed me to live this long, I'm assuming I'll be okay and I'm not to die yet?* The response was, *You will be okay.* I took a deep sigh of relief, but at the same time, I wondered if I was really communicating with a spirit or if I was going crazy. How could I keep having some kind of telepathic communication with something I couldn't see or touch?

The doctors came back into the room and told me I was too sick and needed to go to the emergency room. I explained I didn't have medical insurance and had no intention of going to the ER. They told me that if my condition should worsen in any way, I had to go to the ER regardless if I had insurance or not or I could die. The next day, they called from the walk-in clinic and asked how I was doing. As I was slowly getting better, it was decided I didn't have to go to the ER. Another two weeks passed, and I was finally starting to heal and regain some strength.

My Friend

It was now March of 1993, and my daughter was nine months old. My dear friend who had come to my house many times to help with the kids, laundry, dishes, and food was now ordered bed rest due to complications with her second pregnancy. I was just strong enough to put the children in the car and drive fifteen minutes to her house. By the time I arrived at her house, I was exhausted and needed to lie down to rest. My friend's mother-in-law was staying with them to help care for their four-year-old son as well as caring for my friend. As we were both lying down to rest, my friend on one couch and I on the other couch, her mother-in-law would feed us all peanut butter sandwiches while the kids happily played. We would laugh at how comical the situation was, and the laughter helped us both cope and heal. Always make sure to look at things on the bright side and be thankful for what you can do and have been given in life.

This poem sums up the months I spent in the rocking chair.

"The Rocking Chair"

I go from my bed to the rocking chair.
I go from the rocking chair to my bed.
My head, it pounds when I stand up.
My eyes, they can't focus.
I almost faint while walking to the other room.

The rocking chair is where I sit.
I spend hours in the rocking chair.
I spend days in the rocking chair.
I spend weeks in the rocking chair.
I spend months in the rocking chair.

The rocking chair is black.
It is covered with soft black cushions.
The frame is made of metal.
It is comfortable.
It leans slightly backward.
The meads fold out from underneath.
It makes a footstool.

I sit in the rocking chair.
I hold my infant.
I watch my two boys play.
My parents have gone home.
My mother-in-law has gone home.
My husband is at work.
Now it's just me.
Me, my children, and the rocking chair.

My thoughts are wandering.
I'm so weak.
I wish I would just die.
I wonder why God let me live and feel such pain?
I'm scared of my own thoughts.
I wonder if I will survive.
I tell myself to not question it.
I tell myself to not have these thoughts.
I tell myself to concentrate on healing.
I visualize my body being well.
The soothing music is playing on the stereo.
The CD, it plays non-stop.
I know the score by heart.
The music, it's healing my body.

I imagine being in Hawaii.
I imagine feeling the soft sand between my toes.
I imagine playing with my family on the beach.
I tell myself I'm getting stronger.
I tell myself I'm getting healthy.
I tell myself to only have positive thoughts.
I sing to the baby.
I meditate.
I pray to God to make me healthy.

I'm too weak to do much.
I sit in the rocking chair.
I wonder if today is a day when one of my friends will visit.
The phone rings.
I answer.
It's one of my friends wondering if I need help.
As much as I would like to say I'm okay,
as much as I would like to say I don't need help,
I accept her offer.
I know I can't do it myself.
I tell her I would be delighted if she can come.

I sit in the rocking chair.
I wait.
I long for her to come.
Someone to talk to.
I feel so alone.

An hour goes by.
I'm still in the rocking chair.
The doorbell rings.
My boys open the door.
My friend and her three-year-old son enter.
The boys are jumping up and down of sheer joy to see their
friend.
They all run down the hallway to play.

My friend takes one look at me.
She looks around the house.
She greets me.
She goes straight to the kitchen.
I want to join her.
I can't.
I'm too weak.

She cleans up the dishes.
She picks up the house.
She puts the laundry in.
I want to tell her she doesn't have to work so hard.
I don't.
I know I can't do it myself.
I feel blessed to have such a good friend.

My dearest friend.
She makes lunch for us.
She brings us all sandwiches and tea.
I sit in the rocking chair.
She sits on the couch.
We eat.
We talk.
We laugh.
She heals me just by being there.

Another day goes by.
I sit in the rocking chair.
I hold my infant, sitting in the rocking chair.
Holding and rocking the infant.
That is all I can do.
All I can do in the rocking chair.

The black rocking chair.
My sitting-daybed.
The chair that healed me.
The rocking chair.

ACV

Visualization

If you are trying to heal or accomplish something in life, visualize it already being what you want it to be. I visualized myself as already being healthy and playing on the beach, not as in the process of healing. It's important to create the vision of what you want the outcome to be in the present moment as we to a certain extent create our reality. Your thoughts manifest into reality. If you think poorly of yourself, you will most likely have low self-esteem. If you think highly of yourself, you will most likely have good self-esteem. Think about how you view yourself and your life.

MESSAGE | Watch your thoughts; you create what you think. Use your thoughts to create the outcome you want.

Exercise: Write down what you want to create in your life. Tape this paper to your desk, fridge, mirror, or anywhere you will see it several times per day. If you would like to become a successful salesperson, then visualize yourself as already being this person. If you want to become a better runner, visualize yourself as the best runner you can think of. Create in your mind that you are already the person you are trying to become. Practice this every day.

3

THE AFTEREFFECTS

The Mystery Watches

I started to notice how the lights would start flickering when lying down to read stories to my children. One evening, my four-year-old said, "Mom, why do the lights always blink when you read us stories but never when Dad read us stories?" I told him it was most likely due to a loose connection or something wrong with the electrical cord. Though I thought it was kind of mysterious myself.

In March of 1993, when my daughter was about nine months old, I decided to get a new watch. My old one had stopped working shortly after my brush with death, NDE, the previous summer. I was excited about the possibility of finally being strong enough to venture out to a store to get a new one.

One day, on my way home from my friend's house, I decided to stop at Target. I had just enough strength to walk into the watch department, which was luckily located right inside the entrance. I quickly picked out a watch and paid to avoid standing still too long, which still made me feel faint. After wearing the watch for a few days, it stopped. I thought it was odd, as it was brand new, and decided to exchange it for another one. Again, I mustered up the strength for another quick trip to Target. The lady at the return counter thought it was strange it had stopped as well, as no other watches had been returned. I picked out another one, the same kind I had just returned, and left the store. After a few days, this watch also stopped. I went back to Target to exchange the watch and the lady at the return counter again stated it was strange, as they had not received any other returns. I told her I would pick out a different brand this time and that maybe there was some kind of problem with the manufacturing or quality control process for the brand I had picked previously.

After a few days, this watch also stopped. I told my friend what was happening, and she looked at me and said, "It's not the watch, honey; it's you!" I looked at her with a surprised look, as it hadn't occurred to me that maybe I was the one causing it to malfunction. We both had a good laugh as we realized what was going on. I now understood it wasn't the watch that had a problem—it was me. As I was too embarrassed to go back to the same Target, I decided to return the watch at a different store. Needless to say, I didn't get another watch.

When my daughter was around three years old, I had about sixteen watches in my drawer. I would only purchase a watch with a second hand, as this was the quickest way I could tell if it was working. I kept all the watches in my top drawer to see if any would start up again, as this sometimes happened. The watches that had restarted would work for a few days or sometimes up to two weeks and then stop. I kept rotating them this way for years. After one year, my watch would work for about one month. After two years, it would work for about two months, and so on. It took me twelve years to have my watch tick for twelve months almost to the exact day. After so many years of struggling with my health and electrical interference, I was finally feeling well, and the fact that the watch had lasted an entire year made me feel like I had regained my health and normal life again. At this time, I declared myself healed and stopped wearing watches for a while. Life sometimes seems mysterious, as we are unable to offer a scientific explanation to something we are experiencing. Our existence on earth is delicately intertwined with all that is, and we don't have to or need to understand how everything works. Life is more complex and divine than we can imagine. What matters is what we learn from these experiences and how we integrate them into our life.

The VCR, TV, and Vacuum Cleaner

When the children wanted to watch a video, the VCR would often not turn on if I came too close. I would have to stand in the doorway of the room trying to instruct my six-year-old to push the play button.

Around my daughter's first birthday, I walked through the living room, and as I passed the television, it turned on. I immediately thought the kids must be playing a trick on me with the remote control, but the remote was on the table and the kids were playing outside with their friends. My next thought was that someone else must have the same TV and remote control as we did and assumed that was how the TV had turned on. I was determined to find the cause and went to ring eight of my closest neighbors' doorbells to see if anyone was watching TV. Nobody was watching TV, and most of my neighbors were not even home. I then went back inside our unit, and as I again passed the TV, it turned back on! I now realized it wasn't someone playing a prank on me. It was I who had made it turn on. I felt goosebumps all over my body, and it scared me to think that I was the one causing this to happen. I started to look around the room and for a moment wondered if my grandmother's spirit was in the room and maybe she had made it turn on, as she was the kind of grandmother that would joke with me in all possible ways. I quickly scanned the room with my eyes but wasn't able to see or feel anything. *How is this possible?* I thought. *How could the TV just turn on when I walked by?* I felt anxious, as I didn't have an explanation for what had just happened, and I didn't want to share it with my husband, as I was afraid it would scare him as well.

Another time, about eighteen months after my daughter was born, we had just moved to Long Island, New York, and I was helping my four-year-old with his jacket when the vacuum cleaner all of a sudden turned on about five feet from where we were standing. My four-year-old said with great surprise, "Mom, the vacuum just turned on by itself!" Not wanting to scare him, I stated it must have some sort of electrical problem. However, the vacuum was brand new at the time; I still have this vacuum cleaner twenty-five years later, and it has never had any electrical problems.

Maybe all these events were electrical problem coincidences, but if they were, why did they only happen to me and not any other family member? The kids got used to me having problems with electricity and would joke as I entered their room that they needed to hide the Nintendo game as I may "kill" it! However, there was some truth to their joking.

There were many changes that were taking place, both psychological and physiological. The electrical interference I was experiencing is now understood to be a common phenomenon with people who have experienced an NDE. The electrical interference subsided over the years, which I'm very thankful for, as I've learned that some people may experience problems throughout their life. The aftereffects of someone coming close to death have been studied all over the world, and there are good resources on www.iands.org which show the psychological and physiological aftereffects that are now known to be common.

Teeth, Hair, and Gratitude

It was spring of 1993, and I had kept improving in my strength and stamina since the previous summer and was wondering why all my teeth were suddenly loose. I was reminded of how it felt when I was six years old and my first teeth were about to fall out. I was afraid I was going to lose my teeth and become toothless at the young age of thirty-four. The thought scared me. The fact that I had always had access to medical and dental care made me realize how grateful I should have been all those years. It was a privilege I had taken for granted. My life was a constant roller-coaster of realizing gratitude and experiencing pain and fear. I kept focusing my mind on gratitude, which helped reduce my worrying.

When we worry about something and then redirect the thoughts to gratitude, we make a shift internally, allowing the fear to subside. For example, if you worry about not being able to pay your rent next month, redirect your thoughts to the fact that you have healthy children, a happy marriage, or whatever you can be grateful for, and the worry will be lessened. There is always something you can be grateful for. Even the smallest things can bring gratitude like the fact that you have shoes to wear that day or you have mittens to keep your hands warm.

By January 1994, one and a half years since my NDE on July 10, 1992, and nine months after I had noticed my teeth felt loose, I finally had the strength to visit the dentist. I arrived in Port Jefferson, Long Island, to my dentist's office and found a very nice man in his fifties with silver-gray hair. I immediately felt at ease, as he instilled professionalism and knowledge. After examining my teeth, he jumped in front of me with that same serious look I had gotten used to from all previous doctors, and he said in a worried voice. "All your teeth are loose! What is going on?" I explained what had happened and that my teeth were a lot better now than they were a year ago. He suggested I take a calcium supplement in order to improve the strength of my bones and teeth. One of my wisdom teeth had rotted and had to be extracted. He patiently worked with me and restored my teeth one by one over the next few years.

By 1998, we were being moved back to California and all my teeth had taken hold except for three. When I went to see my new dentist, he had the same reaction as my dentist in New York five years earlier. He jumped in front of me and stated, "Three of your teeth are loose; what is going on?" I told him that was good news! How you interpret a situation is based on your own frame of reference.

I was also experiencing problems with my hair during this time, and as I went to get a haircut, the haircutter jumped in front of me and said, "What is going on? Your hair just breaks in half when I comb it!" It seemed like wherever I went, I was greeted by the same surprised and worried statements. We decided to cut my hair short to help it heal.

I would not recommend to anyone to follow my example of just trusting the Universe that you will heal. If you are struggling with your health, find a good doctor you can trust and work with. Many times, it doesn't matter what kind of doctor he or she is as long as you trust him/her. We are all doctors, MD, NMD, DO, etc. Just find one you like, and you can work with that practice regarding the medicine that you need help with. Someone you can trust, resonate with, and feel comfortable with is an important part of the healing process.

Bruises
By May 1993, I again fell ill with a chest congestion and was now also battling with my teeth and hair problems. My husband

was told we would get insurance July 1 as he had again received a better job offer and was now working for a big corporation. I put the three kids in the car and drove to the doctor. When I had changed the baby's diaper the day before, I accidentally hit my hip against the baby's changing table. Normally this would give rise to a small bruise about the size of a dime or possibly a nickel. My hip, on the other hand, had a bruise about four by six inches wide and spanned my entire hip. The bruise was colored deep purple and red, and as I looked at the size and color, I knew something was terribly wrong. Oddly enough, I was feeling better than I had for the previous nine months, but I now understood that my loose teeth and fragile hair were related to a bigger problem. I remembered how the doctors had asked me if I had AIDS or leukemia a few months ago, and it made me realize that something was wrong with my blood that was causing all these symptoms.

When I arrived at the doctor's office and he raised my shirt to listen to my chest, he saw the large bruise on my hip and immediately jumped in front of me. His face turned serious as he looked me straight in the eye. "How did you get that bruise?" he asked. I told him how I had accidentally bumped into the baby's changing table the day before. He had a look of disbelief on his face and quickly turned around and raised the shirts on all my three children, now ages almost seven, four and a half, and almost one. There were no bruises on my children, and I told him again I was telling him the truth. I was worried he would think my husband was abusing us and maybe report us to social services. I again told him in a calm voice what had happened during the past year, and as he couldn't find any bruises on my children, he calmed down. I took a deep breath, as he finally seemed to believe me. He now seemed more concerned about my health and told me we needed to run some labs STAT. I told him I understood something was wrong but also that I was concerned that if I had a blood test I would most likely not be able to get insurance July 1 due to a pre-existing condition. I also told him how I was actually feeling much better than I had all year and had the strength to put all the children in the car and drive myself to see him. He sighed, as he knew the insurance problem to be true, but still wrote up all the labs and handed them to me.

As we left, I ripped up the labs and buried them in the trash-can in the hallway. My oldest child, aware of what I was doing, said, "Mom, aren't you supposed to do those labs?" I told him the doctor just meant I could do the lab test if I needed them and that he had given me medicine to help me get better. I then quickly used my early childhood education skills and redirected their thought process and told them we were going to get ice cream. Knowing they were going to get ice cream made them all forget what was going on, and they all ran, excited, toward the car. I took a deep sigh of relief but was afraid my oldest child was going to spill the beans to his dad. Thankfully he didn't, and I told my husband I had bronchitis and had been given antibiotics and would soon get better.

My husband was, of course, concerned about the bruise and kept telling me it was not normal. He wanted to take a picture of it and kept saying I would want it later in life. However, I never allowed him to take the picture of the bruise, as I never wanted my kids to know how sick I had been and thought I would never want to look back or be reminded. I was so focused on the present, healing, and looking forward and seeing myself healed and fully functioning. In retrospect, now that I'm a physician, I would have liked to have a picture of it! Sometimes we should listen to others' advice.

New York

It was October of 1993, and we were being moved to New York for my husband's job. I was just strong enough to walk to the gate at the airport. I remember my husband saying, "We should have gotten you a wheelchair," as he could see I was struggling just walking the distance to the gate. My bruises were getting smaller and were now only about one to two inches in diameter and were more bluish-looking than purple.

After being in New York for one month, I came down with strep throat and went to the doctor. When he was taking my blood pressure, he said, "Your blood pressure is seventy over fifty! Are you feeling like you are going to faint?" I of course lied and said, "No, I feel fine." After all, this was how I always felt, and I was feeling better then than I had all year. However, the doctor was concerned, gave me the same stern look all previous physicians had, and wrote up blood labs for me, which I then promptly discarded of in the trashcan as I was leaving the office. This was now becoming habit after visiting a doctor. Now that I'm a doctor myself, I know this was not a smart thing to do, but this seemed to be the right course of action at the time. I didn't trust any doctor after what had happened, and I had completely lost faith in the medical establishment. I was lucky that nothing worse ever came of the situation. If your doctor orders labs, do them. Your doctor is trying to look out for you. Don't follow my poor example of being a non-compliant patient. Do your labs. Things will work out; they always do.

This pattern went on for the next five years. I would get sick two to three times per year and switch doctors each time, as I was afraid of going back to the same doctor who had ordered labs that I had disregarded. I became a very good squatter during these years, as if I put my knee on the floor to help my children tie their shoes, I would get a bruise covering my knee. I struggled for the next five years with feeling dizzy and poor stamina.

I wasn't able to walk through Costco without sitting on a shelf to rest. My children were used to my behavior and didn't think anything of it. After all, it had been like this since they were very young. I kept timing my grocery store shopping so I would avoid the lines at checkout during the busier hours. There were even times when I would have to leave the store and grocery cart behind. Sometimes customers would approach me asking if I was okay. I would assure them each time that I was fine, as I knew I had time before things would start to fade in my vision, forcing me to sit down and put my head between my legs.

I wasn't able to stand up long enough to cook dinner for my children. I remembered my ninety-year-old grandmother who had a stool in the kitchen so she could sit while she was cooking. I purchased a tall wooden stool just like the one she had so I also could sit down while cooking dinner for the children. I wondered how I could possibly be in my thirties feeling the same way as my old grandmother in her nineties. I avoided questioning myself, and I kept redirecting my thought process to visualizing myself as strong and healed.

The Soul

I was going through a difficult time both in the sense that I was trying to understand my experience of having been outside my body as well as being physically ill. I had a sense of not being fully back in my body. It was as if there were two separate parts to me: my body and my soul. I could feel the difference between the two as if they existed separately but were supposed to be joined together as one. I didn't feel "whole." It was as if my soul and body weren't merged as one. I felt as though my soul was constantly trying to rise out of my body. Every time

I had this feeling, I would pray silently, *My children need me; please let me stay.*

The best way to explain this would be to think of your body as if it always lived in a car and you wouldn't be able to leave the car until death. Upon the death of the car, the body would just get out of the car and keep on living. Just like the soul gets out of the body upon death and keep living. Life is continuous; it doesn't end when the car or your body dies. I don't know if this feeling of not being whole was due to my NDE or the fact that I was so sick at the time and was walking a fine line between life and death. I felt as though I was functioning at a minimal existence during this time and have been told by a medium that it was as if I were functioning at only 20 percent life force for the five years that followed my NDE. That is certainly what it felt like.

Message | Always focus on gratitude.

Exercise: Make a list every day and write down five things you are grateful for. This is a good exercise that will help you see the positive things in your life that we otherwise tend to take for granted. You have to write down new things you are grateful for each day, and after a while, you will see even the smallest things bring you gratitude.

4

THE LIGHT, THE MUSIC, AND THE SPIRIT GUIDES

The Visitor

Just after we had moved to New York in the fall of 1993, I woke up in the middle of the night for no apparent reason. All of a sudden, I was aware of a spirit at the end of my bed. I knew it was my uncle. I didn't see him, but I sensed him. I knew he had been battling lung cancer for the past few years but was unaware of his current condition. He was communicating telepathically with me, and I knew instantly he had come to let me know he had passed. He was sending his love to all of us, and I sent him my love as well.

The next day I expected my mother to call, as it was her brother I had communicated with the previous night, but there was no call from my mother. I wondered if I had hallucinated about my uncle, but it all had seemed as real as our regular reality. Three days passed, and my mother finally called. She did her usual small talk first, checking in on us and making sure we were all okay. She then continued and said something sad had happened. I told her my uncle, her brother, had passed away three days ago. My mother became silent. After a long pause, she said, "How did you know?" I told her about his visit, and she told me I was just like her own mother, who had always known when friends and relatives had passed. I'm sure many of you have had similar experiences. Don't ignore them. Trust them. You were born with these intuitive abilities.

A few weeks after my uncle's spirit had visited me, I lay awake one night, pondering how you can still exist when you are outside your body. How did this work? How could my uncle visit me after he died? How could I communicate with him? How was this all possible? There were days when I questioned if I was going crazy. I would talk to my friend who had come to my rescue when I had been bound to sitting in the rocking chair the first year after my daughter was born, and she would assure me I wasn't going crazy and had just had spiritual experiences. She kept telling me I would eventually come to terms with it. Even though I was raised Lutheran in Sweden, I had been an atheist before my NDE and didn't believe there was any life after death, so this experience had really thrown me for a loop. I was in constant processing with what had happened to me during my NDE and what was happening to me in the current moment. After my experience in the ER, I had lost my fear of dying, as I knew I would still exist outside my body even after death. I now saw death as the continuation of life, just on "the other side." I understood that life is eternal and when you die, you still exist but in a different state and form. However, I was still skeptical and kept questioning if the experience had just somehow occurred in my brain or if the soul survived and was able to communicate after the death of the physical body. Being very scientific, I wanted proof that the soul survives.

The Light, the Music, and the Spirit Guides

It had been a normal day of taking care of the children and dealing with my usual health struggles. As the evening approached, we all went to bed, performing the normal bedtime routine.

In the middle of the night, I woke up feeling weak and dizzy. I took my head off the pillow to lower it onto the mattress in order to increase the blood flow to my head. I was so tired of this existence, and I just wanted to be healthy and normal again. I found myself struggling to keep my soul inside of me, as usual, but within a second, my soul was pulled up and out! For a brief moment, I was floating outside my body but then quickly started to travel through darkness. It all happened so fast, just in a few seconds. I felt like I was flying through black, empty space. My soul was traveling at lightning speed. All of a sudden, I arrived at what I call a mid-station. I was again still me, my soul, without my body. I was in spirit form. Somehow, I knew there were levels below me and above me.

I was stunned to hear the most beautiful music. Music so beautiful it can't be made on the earth-plane. I wondered where this beautiful sound came from and saw a little brown wooden log cabin on my right. I opened the door to look inside to see if the music came from the cabin, but to my surprise, the cabin was empty. I looked to my left and saw another cabin, the exact same cabin I had seen to my right. I opened the door to look inside. To my surprise, this cabin was also empty. I was made aware that the music and a very bright light were coming from behind me. My soul slowly turned around, and I saw the most beautiful white light. The music was coming from the light. The light, so bright and magnificent I don't have words to describe it. There isn't any light on the earth-plane that it can be compared to. There was unconditional love emanating from the light, and it felt as though I were part of it. It was so peaceful, beautiful, and radiant. It enveloped me. I was part of the light. I wanted to stay in it forever. It brings tears to my eyes even today. It is what we come from, carry within us, and will return to. It is sacred. It is divine.

In the bright white light, I could see the outline of angels. As I didn't believe in angels, I was confused as to why I was seeing this. I was seeing things I didn't believe to be true. Why was this happening? Suddenly, there was a spirit guide on my right side that was communicating with another spirit guide diagonally in front and to the left of me using instantaneous telepathic communication. The spirit guide on my right said, *"What is she doing here? She can't be here! She has to go back!"*

As I could understand the communication, I responded telepathically and said, *"No. WAIT! How can this be? How can I be outside my body and still be me? How does this work?"*

The spirit guide on my left said, *"If I told you, you wouldn't remember after going back, but you will remember this."* At this point, an image appeared in front of me, and I saw the earth as if from outer space. There was a silvery glittery grid surrounding the earth. At the time, I thought it looked like a fishnet surrounding the earth; that is what it looked like to me, having grown up laying fishing nets with my grandmother in the Atlantic Ocean. When my grandmother stood up in the rowing boat and lifted the nets out of the ocean, the early morning sun would shine on the water droplets on the fishnet, making it glitter in the sunlight. This grid that I saw around the earth looked like a fishnet glittering in the sun.

The spirit guide on my left said, *"Everything on earth is connected to this grid, and everything on earth is connected to one another."*

After this statement, I was sent back to my body at a rapid speed. I traveled at the same instantaneous speed as I had during my first NDE and was sucked back into my body with the same feeling of a strong vacuum hose. *What just happened?* I thought. *How could I leave my body and have a spiritual experience and then just slip back into my body? How did all this work?* As I lay there in bed trying to digest what had happened, my husband sleeping peacefully next to me, I could hear my two-year-old waking up crying, and I thought to myself, *Okay, so I had to be back in time for her waking up. My children need me; that's why they sent me back!* Feeling weak and groggy, I wandered into her room and lay next to her, at which point she returned to sleep right away. I wondered if she somehow knew I had left and had cried out for me to return. After all, she was one of my anchors to the earth side.

What I didn't understand at that moment was how this spiritual experience would transform my life and put me on a new path.

The light I had seen was magical and so divine that it will stay with me forever. It is a knowing and understanding that I came from the light and will return to the light. There is a sacredness and divinity about the music and the light.

At the time I had this experience, we had a Roland synthesizer, which could create many different sounds. I remember sitting at the synthesizer for hours trying to figure out if there were any sounds that came close to the music I had heard emanating from the angels in the light. The closest sound, though not at all as beautiful as the music I had heard, was the sound called Voxy Women Sing. I called the music Angels Sing and tried to play what I had heard to the best of my knowledge. I tried to write down the score, even though I knew it was not complete, but there was no way to create what I had heard. It seemed impossible to make it as beautiful as the music from the angels. I kept this piece of music for many years, in hopes to maybe later be able to figure out how to make it more complete, but at some point, during my many moves, I decided to let go of it, as I wasn't able to create what I had heard. I needed to let go of it in order to move forward. Life is to be lived in the present, not the past. All we have is this moment.

When I was at the "mid-station" seeing the silvery glittery

grid around the earth, was I experiencing astral travel or having another NDE? As I wasn't in the hospital, there is no physical proof of the condition my body was in at the time of the experience. For many years it bothered me to not be able to prove what my experience was or why I'd had such an experience. I know it wasn't a dream and it was more real than life itself. At this point in my life, it doesn't matter what I call the experience. The only thing that matters is that I had a spiritual experience and how it has affected my life. This experience is what allowed me to understand my purpose and the reason I had incarnated into my current life. It provided me with the foundation for my life work.

If you have had similar experiences, how is it affecting you? Many people have the capacity to astral travel, see, hear, or feel spirits as well as other spiritual gifts but are afraid to talk about it as they worry it may make others think they have a psychological illness. I hope by reading this book you will become more open to talking about your own experiences with your friends and family, as you may learn they have had similar experiences themselves. Life is more divine than we many times acknowledge.

Time

When I moved outside my body, everything became timeless. I struggled with this concept for years after my NDE and read many books to try to understand the concept of time. However, as I'm not a physicist, it was difficult to understand the equations in Stephen Hawking books, and I would skip over them when reading to try to get a better general understanding. I've come to think of time as something that is readily available when accessed. It doesn't matter if it is a past, present, or future event. It is as if all moments are readily available. Time on the earth plane as we perceive it doesn't exist on the spirit side.

Sharing

For many years, I was never able to share my own out-of-body experiences with anyone and only shared them with a few close friends I could trust, as I was afraid people would think I was crazy. It wasn't until a few years ago, summer of 2015, when I attended the Association for Near-Death Studies International Conference in San Antonio, Texas, that I learned many people have seen what I saw which is referred to as the "Grid." I had finally reached a point in my life where I was able to share my own spiritual experiences with other people.

Our lives are all very divine and interconnected, and there are many of us with similar experiences. I believe it is time we start sharing our thoughts with one another in order to understand life and our divine existence regardless of our own religious beliefs and values. By sharing our own journeys, we can reclaim our Divine Feminine, sacredness, and divinity of our own existence. The Divine Feminine exists within all of us. Allow yourself to be intuitive and have experiences. We have been taught to suppress our feelings and instincts, especially in Western culture, so we have lost some of this sacredness and these feminine intuitive abilities, the Divine Feminine. Listen to and trust what you feel in your heart and gut. There is something very sacred about our existence. We are all connected.

Do we actually leave the body when we have these experiences, or do we go within our own body? From reading other books and hearing other people talk at conferences, I've learned that the brain is not involved. The brain surgeon from Harvard, Eben Alexander, who wrote the book *Proof of Heaven: A Neurosurgeon's Journey into the Afterlife*, was in a coma but still had an NDE experience to tell when he woke up. They were monitoring his brain with MRI, but the results showed no activity.

Many people that leave their body can accurately tell what was going on around them and conversations that took place even though they should not have been able to according to our current belief system that if the physical body is not working or dead, you should not be able to have an experience. Yet people do have experiences.

Spirituality, Religion and the Yin Yang of Life

After experiencing my NDEs, I became very spiritual. Not spiritual in the sense of believing that one religion is better than another but that all humankind belong together as one. People wrote the texts for different religions. People decided on what gets to be included in these texts and what does not get to be included. The texts were translated into many different languages that may not have had sufficient word choice to express the original meaning of the text. How can we say that one religion is right or better compared to another religion? Many religions have similar beliefs, but when we don't know anything about a specific religion, it may scare us, and therefore, we refuse to accept religions other than our own.

In the book *Jesus, Buddha, Krishna, and Lao Tzu: The Parallel Sayings* by Richard Hooper, we can see quotes side by side from these four different spiritual leaders. On page 112 under the title "Jesus," the quote reads, "Love your neighbor as yourself." *The Gospel According to Mark; parallels: Matthew, Luke, Thomas.* Then under the title "Krishna," the quote reads: "Recognizing what brings pleasure and pain to oneself, the pure yogi treats others accordingly. Thus, he desires happiness for everyone, sorrow for no one." *The Bhagavad Gita.* Then under the heading "Buddha," the quote reads: "Seeing himself in others, one who is in a state of higher consciousness feels compassion for all beings, and holds only positive thoughts about them." *Doctrinal formulas.* Then finally under the heading "Lao Tzu," the quote reads: "Nothing but good comes to him who loves others as he loves himself." *The Tao Te Ching.* The entire book is filled with quotes like this side by side, and we can see the resemblance between the different belief systems.

Life isn't always fair, and many of the people on earth struggle throughout their lives just to survive each day. Many times, I hear people ask how there can be a God if so many people have to suffer. We forget that we, the people, create the world we live in. We, the people, are in charge of letting people suffer. We, the people, are the only ones that can change what we don't like on earth.

Develop Your Own Spirituality

One way to help you become more spiritual is to listen to your heart more. Be in the present, take time to heal yourself, and take time to just be without all your electronic gadgets and obligations. Take time to sit still and sip a cup of your favorite drink and listen to the birds. Close your eyes and be still for fifteen minutes. These small exercises will change how you feel not just physically, but also emotionally and spiritually. It doesn't take much time each day to bring your body into a more peaceful state, which will then help you cope with all your daily stress. In order to connect to the spiritual plane, you need to slow down and just exist. When you are constantly busy, you are not allowing yourself time to connect with the Divine Source. You need stillness to connect spiritually and to listen to what your own heart is telling you. Try to stop thinking and just be in the stillness.

Message | Your existence is divine.

Exercise: Have you had spiritual experiences? If so, have you shared them with someone you can trust? As we are spiritual, intuitive creatures, most of us have had intuitive moments. Notice when you have a gut feeling about something and trust it. To develop your intuitive senses, pay attention to how you feel and to what your intuition is telling you at all times. It could be something silly like knowing someone is going to call you and then they call you just when you are about to call them. Write down every time something like this happens, and you will soon discover a pattern of your intuitive abilities. Don't ignore or suppress your intuition, and don't let anyone influence you to discount them. Embrace your intuitive self.

5

HOPE

Vacation

It was February of 1996 and my daughter was three and a half years old. I was finally strong enough to go on vacation. It had been a long three years of feeling stranded and abandoned in the house. Finally, some hope that I was on the road to recovery. We decided to take the kids to Vermont to teach them how to ski. I was exuberant.

Dressed in my snow pants, down jacket, and winter boots, I slowly walked across the terrain toward my skis, which were leaning against the ski rack at the bottom of the slope. As I walked, the snow made a squeaky sound under my feet which made my whole body smile. As my muscle tone was poor from not having been active the past few years, my ski boots felt like bowling balls around my legs, but it didn't matter, as I was too excited to just be outside surrounded by the beautiful snow-covered mountains. As I put my skis on, I felt as excited as a child on Christmas morning. *Nothing lasts forever*, I thought. You may go through valleys in life, but eventually, things will get better. Just being able to be on the mountain and breathing in the fresh air, seeing all the happy children and adults playing in the snow, made me feel so alive and happy. It made me realize how precious each moment is. Even though I had skied many times in my life, I now realized how

I had been preoccupied with what I was going to do next and forgot to treasure the current experience. Slow down and just breathe. Enjoy the moment.

"Hope"

Hope is when you lie awake in your bed at night,
listening to the soothing sounds of your newborn infant sleep,
your hands and feet are ice cold,
your body is freezing,
you feel your blood pressure falling,
you feel faint while lying down,
and you pray,
you pray to still be alive in the morning.

.

Hope is when you hear a voice in the middle of the night,
a voice telling you,
telling you, you will be okay.

Hope is when you are strong enough
to stand up long enough,
long enough to make lunch for your children,
long enough to take your children on a walk,
long enough to make the trip to the grocery store for a
gallon of milk.

.

Hope is when you are strong enough to go on vacation,
strong enough to ski down a bunny slope,
strong enough to have some fun.

Hope is when you are lying on the ski hill camouflaged in snow,
laughing, staring at the ice cold blue sky,
laughing because you feel like a beached whale,
laughing because you're not sure you can get yourself up,
laughing because you realize the comedy in your mishap.

Hope is when you are able to see the humor in your inabilities,
your inability to physically functioning at a normal level,
to see the humor in the situation your inability has caused,
to be able to see the humor and laugh,
laughing together with your snow-covered three-year-old
wearing a bunny hat,
laughing, reminding you that life is merry.

Hope is when you are able to see the joy in your life,
the joy of being alive,
the joy of being with the ones you love,
the joy of your family and friends,
the joy each day brings.

Hope is when you realize nothing in life is important except
all the lives in it.
Hope is when you never stop believing.
Hope is what life is built on.

ACV

New Beginnings

I was finally on the mend after having been accustomed to feeling faint and tired for five to six years. It all changed the year we moved back to California in May of 1998. I was now able to function and walk through the stores without feeling weak or dizzy but would still get sick easily, as my immune system was still not optimal yet.

In August of 1999, seven years after the birth of my daughter, I again came down with pneumonia. The doctor, a very nice female, told me I was way too sick for it being August and that we needed to do some blood work. I thought this scenario was never going to end. I explained we were soon to move to San Francisco, and I was sure most of it was caused by asthma and allergies in Orange County in Southern California. I promised to have lab work done in San Francisco should I not get better. I was again given antibiotics, steroids, and inhalers to overcome my pneumonia, and the lab work she gave me was again discarded of in a trashcan on my way out of the building.

It wasn't until after our move to San Francisco in 2000 that I finally was straight with a doctor. It was ten years after my daughter was born that I finally had my first lab work which showed just slightly below normal levels of white and red blood cells as well as platelets. I told the doctor my story, and he told me that most likely I had experienced what is called idiopathic aplastic anemia. Not knowing what those terms meant, I responded with, "Anemia! No, it was worse than just being anemic!" He laughed; I knew I must not have understood what that term really meant. He was about to explain it to me, and I stopped him in the middle of his sentence. I said, "Don't tell me. I don't want to know how bad it was. I will just worry about it returning." He smiled, as he understood. I never looked up what that term meant until I was in medical school. I never wanted to know or understand what it was, as I was afraid of making it somehow return by thinking and worrying about it and just kept focusing on being healthy in the present moment. It didn't matter anymore; all that mattered was that I was well. It was now in my past.

Process

In retrospect, I think part of my thinking helped me get well, and part of me wishes I had processed it all sooner. Again, here is the yin and yang of our existence. There is never a right or wrong way in what we do; it's all just a process. At the end of our life, this process will have served a purpose for our soul to grow. Our life is like walking on a hiking trail with some trails that are steeper and harder and other trails that are easier to walk. You choose your different roads to take in life, but in the end, they all lead to the same destination.

By being in tune with your heart and what your soul desires versus what your mind tells you, you are more likely to find happiness on your journey in life. Listen to your gut feelings and choose your path based on what you truly resonate with. Ask yourself if what you are doing in life makes your heart sing or if it makes your heart feel like its living in a cage. There is always free will in your life, so listen to your heart and choose your paths wisely.

Whenever I had to explain my past medical history to a doctor, it was as if I opened a can of worms and all the worries about the illness returning would resurface. I would then have to re-focus my thoughts and visualize myself as healthy for the next few days in order to alleviate the worries. Maybe you have had traumatic experiences or struggled with your health in life and are familiar with how our mind works when reminded of the event. This is a poem I wrote about this struggle.

"The Monster and the Wound"

A new pain.
A new ache.
A visit to a new doctor.
The wound, it opens up.
The monster, it surfaces.
The story of the past, unfolded once again.

The illness of the past, described in words.
Words that aren't sufficient to describe what once occurred.
Words that try to tell a story of sickness and healing.
Words that bring pain to the soul.
Words, so powerful to the person using them,
yet for the person receiving them,
they are mere words with no feelings or emotions attached.

The story of the past,
triggering the opening of a wound that was healed.
Like worms crawling out of a can,
like a monster emerging from the deep.
The monster that was safely tucked away under the sand,
under the sand, at the bottom of the ocean floor.
The monster of sickness.
The monster of fear.
The monster of the unknown.

Is the wound going to open up?
Is the monster once again going to take over my body?
Is my body once again going to battle for survival?
Am I once again going to wake up from dreams
where I'm dying?

It is all about taming the monster and healing the wound.
The fight of having or having had a disease.
The fight of not knowing what lies in the future.
The fight with your brain to not think about what you have
or had.
The fight to overcome your physical ailment.
The fight to overcome the mental burden of always
questioning.
The fight to keep your spirits high.
The fight to stay well.
The fight with pain.
The fight to keep going.

To describe the past opens a wound in the moment.
To live in the moment heals the wound of the past.

The monster and the wound once again return to their
tucked-away places.

ACV

MESSAGE | Never ever give up hope.

Exercise: When you feel like you are stuck and hopeless, remember that your experiences in life are transient. Nothing lasts forever. When you feel hopeless, take time to ground yourself. Sit still and just breathe. Notice how many beautiful things you can see around you. Replace your thoughts of hopelessness with gratitude. Do something nice for yourself. It could be taking a bath, journaling, drinking a cup of tea and lighting a candle, drawing, watching a movie, or talking to a friend. Allow yourself to get a little pampered and feel special. There is only one of you, and you are magnificent and special the way you are. Treasure that!

6

CLAIRVOYANCE

After my NDEs, I started seeing things before they happened. I had become clairvoyant. Many people are born this way or the ability evolves during their life without having come close to death. I believe we all, to a certain extent, have these capabilities, but most of us are not taught to evolve this part of ourselves. I've met many people from around the world who are very gifted in these capacities and have allowed themselves to develop their intuitive abilities. To give you some examples of how it evolved for me, I'll tell you a few stories. Maybe you have had similar experiences but have discounted them as coincidences.

The Accident

Right after I woke up one morning around the year 2001, I experienced a clairvoyant message. I was shown three images in successive order. The first image was of a large horizontal black scratch across the sliding door on the passenger side of our van. I understood the image was showing me that we had been in an accident. In the second image, I was shown two of my children in the car, one in the front passenger seat and the other in the back seat. I knew the children were my two younger children who were at the time about twelve and nine years old. In the third image, I saw myself leaving a note on the windshield of a black sedan car. I knew that none of us had been injured, and

I wasn't aware of any information regarding the passengers of the black sedan. I thought it was very odd that I was leaving a note on the black car and wondered, *Where was the driver of the black car? Had the driver been injured and taken to a hospital? But if that driver was injured, shouldn't there have been a police officer at the site?* I told my two younger children about my vision, and we discussed the several possibilities where we could be involved in an accident. We all felt it was most likely going to happen if we were making a left turn and had oncoming traffic that could collide with the right side of our car. There was only one likely intersection for such an accident that we could think of.

As I drove them to San Francisco every day for their ballet lesson, we would take the Bay Bridge across the water to San Francisco. As we would exit the bridge and head down on to the surface streets, we would make a left turn, which had oncoming traffic. For about ten days, we arrived at the traffic light of the suspected accident intersection and the children looked anxiously out of their windows to make sure there was no oncoming traffic that could hit us.

After about ten days of suspenseful driving, we arrived at Walnut Creek, our local shopping center. We had done some shopping at the bookstore, and when exiting the garage, there was a big truck parked on my left offloading boxes. I tried to squeeze by the big truck and out on to the narrow street making a right turn, and there were several cars in line trying to enter the parking area. As I was turning right on to the street, the right side of my car, the passenger van door, scraped the black sedan that was parked on the street. I immediately knew this was the accident I had seen and got out of my car to look at the damage. As I saw the black horizontal scratch across my van door, I tilted my head backward toward the blue sky, threw my arms up in the air, and started to laugh out loud hysterically.

The scratch on my door matched the image I had been shown two weeks earlier perfectly. *Finally*, I thought, *no more worrying!* The person offloading boxes on the truck as well as the pedestrians on the sidewalk and drivers in nearby cars just stared at me. They must have thought I was crazy, as I was laughing at my own accident! I left a note on the windshield of the black sedan, which was parked, to let the owner know my information. Nobody was hurt—it was just material damage—and we were all relieved the accident was over and we could stop worrying. Now I understood why I had not been shown the driver of the black sedan! Life really isn't that serious. Sometimes you just have to laugh at your own mistakes and mishaps!

Remote Viewing

I was at home in our kitchen about to start preparing dinner. My son, now about eighteen years old, had borrowed my car, as he drove his girlfriend and my daughter to class in San Francisco. All of a sudden, I saw my children in the car making a U-turn at the light on the Embarcadero in front of the Ferry Building. A large truck was approaching from the opposite direction and was accelerating in order to go through the light on a yellow to red signal. I saw my son in the car assuming the truck was going to stop. I saw the light changing and the truck accelerating. As he started to turn, I could see how he saw the truck approaching at fast speed, and he stepped on the gas to accelerate as fast as he could to avoid getting run over by the truck. I saw my daughter's body being hurled in the back seat by the sudden turn of the car. The truck missed them by a few inches! I was instantly thrown into a panic mode. It was as if I were watching the scene playing out in front of me standing on the sidewalk! I tilted my head backward toward the ceiling and the sky and said out loud, "Thank you, God! That was close!" My adrenalin was pumping, and I felt as shaken as if I had been present at the scene. I was relieved knowing they were okay, as I could see their car speeding off down the street. It took me a while to calm down, and I had to sit at the kitchen counter to catch my breath.

As the kids came home later that evening, after they had finished eating, my daughter said, "Mom, we almost got hit by a truck."

I looked at her and her brother and said, "Yes, on the Embarcadero making a U-turn at the light by the Ferry Building! I saw you!" Their jaws dropped, but at the same time, they were not surprised, as they were used to me having these kinds of experiences.

Have you ever experienced something like this? How can we see things when not even being present? Is this a skill we all have but don't know how to develop?

My Father

My brother called me from Sweden in mid-March of 2000 to let me know my father had experienced an ischemic stroke. I asked him if I should get on a plane right away to visit him, but my brother, a surgeon, ensured me that our father was doing well and that I could wait a few days before coming. We booked tickets for the children and me to visit him the following week. Within a day or two, my brother again called to let me know Dad was doing well and had been moved on to a rehabilitation floor for further recovery.

The children were now ages thirteen, eleven, and eight years old, and we went to the bookstore to get some books on tape for the children for the long flight to Sweden. As we were shopping, I kept seeing an image of a white coffin. It was decorated with beautiful deep red flowers, and I saw the coffin at a right angle and from slightly above. I told my husband about the image that kept appearing and that I knew it was my dad's coffin. My husband assured me I was just worried about him and reminded me that my dad was doing well and had been moved on to the rehabilitation floor at the hospital. Neither my brothers nor my mother called us over the weekend to let us know how he was doing. I later found out that I had started seeing the images of the coffin around the same time my dad had collapsed in the hospital and taken a turn for the worse. However, my family, knowing that I was arriving soon, didn't want to worry me and therefore didn't call me. I cried several times during the weekend, as I felt my father was going to pass.

Two days later, we boarded our flight, and as we arrived the next day after twenty-two hours of traveling, I was surprised to see my sister-in-law greeting us at the airport instead of one of my brothers. She had a pale and worried look on her face and said, "Hurry, we have to go now!" I asked if I had time to use the restroom; she responded no, that we had to leave right away, that time was of essence. We all quickly walked to her parked car, and as soon as we were all buckled in, she stepped on the gas and drove us as quickly as possible to the hospital. I worried about my father during the car ride and wondered if I would make it in time. My sister-in-law filled me in on the details of what had happened since Friday. I now understood why I had seen the coffin. I knew that the images I had seen were true. It was as if the spirit world had prepared me for what was coming. As we arrived, one of my older brothers greeted me at the entrance and took me upstairs in the elevator to the room where my father was. My mother whispered in my dad's ear that I had arrived. My father opened his blue eyes for a second to meet my eyes. This was the last time my eyes met his. I can still see this image clearly in my mind. During the next hour, we held his hands; I kissed his forehead and stroked his body as we watched him peacefully transition and leave the earth plane behind. It was an hour filled with sadness, gratitude, peace, and love.

During the next few days, I helped my mother arrange the funeral, and we went to the flower store to order flowers. The florist in the store gave my mother a huge binder with about eight pictures per page of flower arrangements. My mother carefully took her time to look through the binder and finally narrowed down her choices to two different flower arrangements. One of the arrangements was exactly the same as I had seen in my vision. She asked me which one I thought would be best for my father's funeral. I told her she knew my father best and to choose the one she thought he would have chosen. She chose the exact flower arrangement I had seen in my vision. I again wondered how this could be. Was it all predetermined?

A few more days passed, and we were now ready for the funeral service. As we arrived at the chapel, I was asked to sit on the right side of the circular room on the second-level tier. The view of the coffin was at a right angle and from slightly above, the exact same way I had been shown in the image when at the bookstore. All the previous funerals I had attended the coffin had been placed either horizontally or vertically to my view. I had seen it on an angle and slightly from above because the room was circular with tiered seating, which had been completely unknown to me.

We are all connected to one another, and many of you may have had similar experiences. We all experience gut feelings about what is right or wrong, and sometimes we know when someone is to leave the earth plane. Never ignore these feelings and messages. Develop your intuitive abilities by acknowledging what you see, hear, or feel.

Clairaudience

As I was cooking dinner in our kitchen, I "heard" someone

communicating with me telepathically. The voice was saying the name of a relative and the words "gallbladder, liver, spleen." The message wouldn't stop and kept repeating itself. I told my two younger children who were sitting at the kitchen counter what I was experiencing.

My daughter said, "Well you better call his mom and tell her!"

I picked up the phone and dialed the mother of the child's name I had heard. I knew that the person in the message had recently undergone an appendectomy, and I wondered why I kept hearing the message about his other organs. When I spoke with the mother, she said she had recently returned home to the east coast after being with him during the surgery and that her son was on the mend. I told her about the message I was receiving and to check on her son to make sure he was okay. She immediately called him, and he told her that he had started to feel worse after she had left. She immediately booked a flight and flew back out to one of the western states where he was attending college. As she took her son back to the hospital, they found he was experiencing an infection after the appendectomy causing his gallbladder to fail as a result, and he ended up in surgery to have it removed. A few months later, he also lost his spleen in a freak accident, when he accidentally got kicked by his horse while helping a lady catch her dog which was off-leash and attacking his horse. He ruptured his spleen and ended up having to have a splenectomy. Luckily, nothing happened to his liver and it's still with him after all these years! Sometimes we receive signals or warning signs; listen to them!

The Red Truck

Sometimes the image or vision that I receive will be something brief and is usually a warning. A few weeks back when I was getting ready to leave and drive to Phoenix, which was about a two-hour drive from where I was living at the time, I was shown an image and heard a message. The image was of a red truck swerving into the left lane on the highway with the telepathically communicated message: *"Watch out for the red truck!"* I tilted my head to the heavens and thanked my spirit guides for the message and told them I would be on alert.

As I was driving, I kept my eyes open for a red truck. After about an hour of driving, I was about to pass another truck. I noticed that this truck was red, and I remembered the warning I had received earlier that morning. I waited for the car in front of me to pass the truck completely, leaving enough room behind him for me to pass the truck safely. As we were passing a section that had guardrail on the left side, I kept my position behind the truck and waited for an opportunity to pass after the guardrail section had ended. This would leave me room on the shoulder in case the truck swerved into my lane. As the car in front of me cleared the truck and I was getting ready to accelerate to pass him, the truck suddenly swerved into the left lane in front of me! If I had been passing him at that moment, he would have hit my car and pushed me off the freeway. I took a deep breath and again thanked my spirit guides for the warning and waited for him to correct his truck and was all the way back in the right lane before I passed him. I let out a loud *"Woohoo"* scream in the car, as I was happy, I was safe, and the worry had passed.

Dreams

Have you ever had a dream and told someone about it and then later found out that the place exists where you went in your dream? By telling people about your dreams or writing them down, you can then later go back and verify if you had a dream about the place or if you are experiencing déjà vu. I've had dreams like this, and I like to keep a dream journal for this reason so I can later go back and see if I actually did have a dream about a place or if it is just my memory playing tricks on me creating a déjà vu experience.

Not only do we dream when we sleep but it is also important to have dreams during the day. Do you dream of one day meeting a special person, getting a new job, or going back to school? I have many dreams, and one of my dreams is to be on *The Ellen DeGeneres Show* and *SuperSoul Sunday* with Oprah Winfrey. I will never give up on these dreams, and I hope that someday I will make it on to their shows!

What are you doing to make your dreams come true? Don't sit back and wait for it to happen; you have to take action in order for your dreams to become reality. Just taking small steps in the right direction will start to change your path. If you are dreaming of going back to school, start by taking any class at a local community college to get back in the swing of being in school. It doesn't have to be what you want to focus on; it could be an art class or anything that comes easy to you to make the transition less scary as you adjust to school life. Small steps lead to bigger steps as you grow.

The Twelfth Year
The year 2003 to 2004 was the twelfth year after my first NDE, and this year involved processing what happened to me both physically and spiritually from having come so close to death. As I had just focused on visualizing myself being physically well all the prior years, I now needed to process what had happened to me emotionally. I experienced a lot of anxiety this year and would wake in the middle of the night sweating, panting and out of breath, dreaming that I was dying and hearing the nurse

yell my blood pressure: *"Fifty over fifteen; HURRY!"*

It wasn't that I was afraid to die but the fear that my children would grow up without a mother. I would wake up with the thought, *I can't die! My kids need me!* My maternal instinct was so strong, and it made me realize how connected I was to my children. I would dream over and over again that I was dying and fighting for my life. During this time, I would also write poems, state out loud that I forgave the doctors for not finding and treating my hemorrhaging sooner, as well as thanking the doctor who had saved my life. I processed a lot of emotions, and I had to learn to let go of the past. Learning to let go of the past was something that had already been a challenge for me, so this experience amplified this learning.

This went on for about a year, and during this time, I also read a lot of books. I always joke that I read half of the San Francisco Public Library that year. I read on average a book a week for about a year. I had stacks of books next to my bed and was reading more than one book at a time. Every time I would walk into the library or bookstore during that year, I would find a book I needed to read. Sometimes, I wasn't even looking for a book for myself but only accompanying a friend. It was as if the book was "talking to me," saying, "Read me," as my mother-in-law used to say. I would randomly pick a book off the shelf and open it to a page in the middle of the book, and my eyes would land just on the right paragraph that contained the information I had been seeking! This would happen over and over again almost on a weekly basis for a year. It was astounding and beyond coincidence. I started to understand the Universe really is divine. There is guidance if we listen. We just need to quiet the mind to hear, see, or feel the guidance.

MESSAGE | Develop your intuitive abilities by acknowledging what you see, hear, or feel.

Exercise: When you have moments of feeling like someone is telling you something or catching a glimpse of something in your mind, tell someone about these moments or write them down in a notebook or on your phone. Keep a list of these intuitive moments so you can go back and verify that you, in fact, did have a premonition about something. When we don't write these moments down or tell someone, we may later question if we really did have knowledge about a future event or if we are experiencing a déjà vu. Don't be discouraged if you get some information wrong in the beginning; just keep practicing.

7

WHERE MY LIFE BEGAN

Kindness

I was born and raised in a suburb of Stockholm, Sweden, which is part of the Scandinavian countries in northern Europe just underneath the North Pole.

I was the kind of kid who would stick up for the less fortunate or bullied kids, and I would literally wrestle some of the boys to the ground and tell them to stay away from a child they picked on. I was also good in sports and was often the person chosen to pick the team for the gym-class sporting event in school. Many times, I would pick a weaker player at the beginning instead of the strongest player just to make that person feel special. I really disliked the way we would pick the team, as the weak players would always be left to be the last ones picked. I always felt awful and my heart would ache for them, as their faces always looked so sad, as they knew they were considered the worst players. Some of these children just weren't good at ball-sports; they were good at other things like riding horses. Sometimes I would pass the soccer ball or basketball to one of the worst kids during gym class just to see a smile light up their face as they felt valued enough to partake in the game. These small gestures were often more important to me than winning the game. Life isn't about winning. Sometimes making someone else happy and feel appreciated is much more important and can literally be life-changing for that person.

When I was in my thirties, my mother met one of my former classmates at the grocery store who was one of the friends and fellow classmates I had fought off the boys for, as they were bullying her for wearing glasses due to a lazy eye. She told my mother to thank me for sticking up for her in fourth grade and how it had changed her life. Small acts of kindness counts! Do what you can in life to help others; you may have a bigger impact on their life than you can imagine.

The Rower

During the summers, we would spend time at the summer home on one of the thousands of islands that the Swedish archipelago consists of. There was no running water, electricity, or phone on the island, which meant we brought drinking water in big plastic containers with us from the city.

My grandmother and grandfather were the first inhabitants on the island, and they had borrowed money to purchase the land and then sold off sections to pay off the loan and were left with just enough money to build a small wooden cabin to use during the summers. Our house, which was built the year I was born, was a five-minute walk through the forest to my grandmother and grandfather's house.

As I got older and was about seven years old, I had finally graduated to become the official boat rower for my grandmother. I was so excited and proud to be able to carry out a task that only my older brother had been able to do. Every evening, my grandmother would lay five nets in the Atlantic Ocean to catch fish for all of us to eat. To be the official rower of the boat, I had to wake early in the morning to meet my grandmother at the dock. My mother would wake me, and I would quickly get out of my bed and pull on my shorts, t-shirt, and orange life preserver. Feeling important, happy, and appreciated, I would run and skip through the forest to my grandmother. Life seemed magical.

Think back to your own childhood; what seemed magical to you then? Do you have any magical moments in your life today? If not, revisit those magical moments from your childhood and create new ones to enjoy in your life today.

Career Choices

I have wanted to be a doctor for as long as I can remember. My dad was a doctor, a family practitioner, and would encourage my older brother to become a doctor. When I told him I wanted to be a doctor as well, he looked at me and said, "You don't want to become a doctor; it takes a long time and you'll be left with high student loans. You should become a nurse." I would tell him I didn't want to become a nurse; I wanted to become a doctor. He didn't mean any harm in telling me this; he was just protective of his little girl, and it wasn't common for girls to become doctors during this time period. Women were supposed to stay home and raise children, and men were supposed to go after their careers.

The school counselors encouraged me to study the sciences in high school, as in Sweden, we major in something in high school. You can major in the sciences, languages, economics, childcare, sports, mechanics, and many more areas to get prepared to take a job upon graduating. I learned that there were only going to be about three girls in the science major class. Being only fifteen years old, I decided I would most likely not have any friends or boyfriends if I attended the science class. I thought I wouldn't be in what was considered the popular group of kids if I went that route, so I decided to major in business and foreign languages to ensure popularity and hopefully boyfriends.

I didn't understand that happiness comes from following

your own heart and not from what you think other people want you to do or trying to find the path of least resistance in order to get an education or make a living. The concept of following your own heart was foreign to me at that time. I think this is still a common problem for our youth today as they struggle with trying to find a career that will ensure a good income as well as secure a job upon graduation. There are so many social pressures on our youth today, and going to college unfortunately does not ensure a good job upon graduation anymore. Listen to your heart. What makes you want to wake up in the morning? Follow that thread to find your path.

Energy Fields

Looking back at my life as a child now, I can see that my spiritual development began all the way back in childhood. All the experiences I had as a child impacted my spiritual development as an adult. Think back to your own childhood. What do you remember? What came to you naturally then? Do you still nurture this innate talent?

One day, when I was about nine years old, I was sitting at the kitchen table staring at the flowers in the vase. My brother pointed out to me that there was a field around the flowers if you looked carefully with sort of squinted eyes. He asked if I could see this white fuzzy field, to which I responded with an enthusiastic yes! "It's the energy field of the flower," I said. I later asked my friend if she could see it, too, whereupon she looked at me and laughed and told me I must be crazy. "There is no field around the flower," she said. The funny part about this story is that today she is a very spiritual woman and a medium capable of communicating with spirits.

Just because you haven't been able to see spirits or auras as a child doesn't mean you won't develop these skills later in life. To a certain extent, we all have these abilities within us. Some have more abilities and some fewer. How much you have isn't important. What is important is that you recognize that you have them. After this experience of asking my friend if she could see the energy field around the flower, I was more cautious about telling people about things I saw. Think back to your own childhood; did you see things you have suppressed and no longer see or notice?

We are all at different stages in our spiritual and emotional development, and sometimes people aren't ready to hear what you want to share, as they are not yet ready to take in your information. The people you are close to all have different agendas and journeys they are on. Don't despair. Stick with *your* journey. The right people will show up to help guide you on your path. Have faith. It doesn't mean you have to give up your current friends; just be tolerant and understand that they are on a different path in life, and it doesn't always match or blend well with the path you are on. Sometimes you need to let go of old friends and find new friends along the way, as this may be part of your own growth. You are walking on your own path of life. They are walking on their path. Sometimes we walk together, and sometimes we walk alone.

Boundaries

My childhood was easy in many ways, but like many people, I experienced inappropriate touching as a child, which occurred over the span of a few years. As my boundaries had been repeatedly violated, though brief in nature, it still took many years for me to heal.

If you have had your boundaries crossed in some way or another, pay attention to how it affects you or affected you at the time. Incidents like this can stay with you for life and may take time to release from your body, mind, and spirit. The trauma is also stored in your cells and tissue, and if you have experienced any kind of trauma, it is important that you work with a counselor or other professional if needed so you can process and let go of any emotions that no longer serve you.

Think about how you treat your child, girlfriend, boyfriend, or other people you are close to. Sometimes what seems innocent to you is not so innocent to the person you are pushing your boundaries on. It doesn't take more than one instance of doing something that is inappropriate to another person to create trauma. The person whose boundaries were crossed may start to no longer trust in other people and will consider them as unsafe. This lack of trust may then transfer over to not trusting people in general when they find themselves in a similar situation that once caused them harm, resulting in them projecting this fear onto other people who are, in fact, good and safe people. The crossing of boundaries creates a fear of the scenario repeating at another time or place and maybe with a different person. It creates an overall distrust.

Children are especially vulnerable, as they may be dependent on the person crossing their boundaries and are not yet equipped to handle situations like this. They may also be threatened by the person to not tell anyone about the incident. They may therefore be afraid of telling someone about their experience and will find different coping mechanisms to deal with the situation.

Many times, the abuse can be verbal. Even teachers can be guilty of verbal abuse toward children. These continuous verbal accusations cause emotional scars that we carry with us for a long time and sometimes our whole life. Adults, as well as children, are abused, and the abuse can take many forms such as mental, emotional, sexual, and physical. Many times, when adults are abused emotionally, they may be told they are incapable, stupid, or can't do anything right as well as called a bitch, cunt, or any other slang word used to put a person down. Women may be raped by their own boyfriends or husbands, or physically hit by people they are close to and live with. Since becoming a physician, I have realized abuse is much more common and widespread than we think. You can't tell by the way a person looks or their appearance what their life story is. Past trauma doesn't look a certain way on the surface of a person. You can't tell by the way a person dresses or their general appearance what they have been through in life. Don't judge people by their cover!

Following are some suggestions on how to protect yourself against having your boundaries crossed and having negative energy sent toward you.

- If you feel your boundaries are being crossed, leave the situation that is making you uncomfortable if possible. Seek help if needed. Speak from your heart, not your mind, when evaluating what is going on. Does the situation resonate love in your heart? If not, you should try to remove yourself from the situation. The person who is crossing your boundaries may be playing with your mind, trying to make you believe it is your fault. Trust your heart and your instinct.

- Set the intention of not taking on the negative energy by telling yourself in your mind the following: *I'm not taking on this negative energy. The negative energy belongs to the person (say the name of the person). My energy is positive and full of love and light.*

- Using your mind, gently scoop the negative energy back toward them. It may sound crazy to you, but try it for yourself to see if the situation improves. The energy that someone gives off with any type of abuse is negative, and by scooping it back toward them, you help protect yourself from this energy. They will feel the negative energy themselves but not necessarily understand what it is they are feeling.

- You can also scoop up the energy and send it out to the Universe to get recycled. As the law of conservation states, "Energy is never created nor destroyed." Recycle it!

There are many ways to help release trauma through various kinds of energy work such as emotional release technique, journaling, as well as working with a counselor or other professional and getting support from friends and the community. Don't suppress your emotions; work to release them and let them get recycled in the Universe. Don't let them manifest physically in your body.

My Most Embarrassing Moment
As American societal norms and parents tend to be stricter about having a boyfriend come over to a girl's house compared to the norms of Swedish society, my boyfriend was very cautious about coming home with me. In Sweden, it is much more relaxed, and the parents typically understand that their kids are going to have sex when they are ready. Most parents I knew felt that it would be safer to let teenagers have sex in their own bedrooms rather than having sex in a car or elsewhere in order to feel safe and use protection.

One evening after we had been to a friend's house, I managed to convince my boyfriend to come home with me. It was already around 11:30 p.m., and I confidently told my boyfriend that my parents were asleep upstairs. We took our shoes off as we entered the apartment and tiptoed into the living room to not wake my parents, or so we thought. There was a glass door into the living room, which divided the living room from the entrance and hallway. When you entered the apartment, you could see directly into the living room through the glass doors.

My boyfriend and I started to make out on the sofa. More and more of our clothes kept coming off our bodies until neither of us had any clothing left. We were now completely naked. As I was lying on my back with my boyfriend on top of me, we heard the key in the front door. We gave each other a look of panic and abruptly stopped making out. Within seconds, I saw my father standing on the other side of the glass door looking at my boyfriend and myself. He was covering his mouth while pointing at us through the glass door and arched backward as he gave off a loud gut belly laughter. I'm pretty sure we surprised him. My boyfriend turned pale and levitated upward and backward off the sofa! A movement that seems impossible to accomplish unless you experience a huge surge of adrenalin. During this process, he hit the floor lamp, which swayed back and forth, and as he was bending forward trying to pull his jeans up, his behind was mooning my father on the other side of the glass door. As my boyfriend was busy trying to pull up his pants, I was completely uncovered and lying naked and exposed to my father's view. As my father continued to laugh, I waved hello with my right hand with a smile on my face. I was so embarrassed and didn't know what else to do. This was definitely the most embarrassing moment of my life! However, it was comical. My father, being a physician and seeing the humor in the event, then walked up the stairs with firm and loud footsteps as if to make a statement that he was going upstairs and we were safe to continue. My boyfriend and I were mortified, and for several days afterward, my father would toast us at dinner and wink at my boyfriend, who would repeatedly turn several shades of red.

It is these types of moments that help shape us in life. My father could have chosen to be angry with us and scold us for our behavior. He could have told me to never have a boyfriend over again. Instead, he laughed and understood us at this age. He knew that we were sexually active, and he would rather have his daughter at home in a safe environment when experimenting and learning about sex than having me in a situation where I would not feel safe and protected. I believe that when we are shown how to deal with these situations in our youth, it helps us become more patient and tolerant with ourselves as well as our own children later in life. The glass is always half full, never half empty. Learn to look at things from a positive perspective.

MESSAGE | What is your journey? Listen to your heart and your own inner wisdom! Don't live to please others; live to please yourself.

Exercise: When you wake up in the morning, ask yourself if you are looking forward to your day. When you go to bed at night, are you excited about tomorrow? If not, then ask yourself what makes you want to wake up the next morning. What makes you "tick"? What inside you could you do all day without being bored? What do you do that makes time fly? When you start paying attention to these things, you will start to understand what your natural talent is. It could be something you think is silly and will never support you; however, if you take small steps to allow yourself to do the things you love, they will eventually lead to greater satisfaction and happiness in your life and may someday become the way you support yourself.

8

THE FIRST TIME I THOUGHT I WAS GOING TO DIE

The Move to the United States

After my American boyfriend and I spent a year studying at Stockholm's University, we decided to get married. A few days after our wedding, I had to say goodbye to my family, as I was moving to the United States. I was both sad and excited. Sad, because I was moving so far away from my family and friends but excited about all the new possibilities and adventures that were waiting. It wasn't easy to make this transition, but I was relieved to be able to live with my husband without having to worry about obtaining a visa.

First Job in the US

As my husband started his studies in summer school, I started my search for a job. I had no idea what I should do, as I was only a sophomore in college and didn't have a degree to show. I did, however, have some work experience, as I had worked in the hospital cafeteria when I was fourteen years old, making sandwiches and working the cash register. I had then taken a job at the clothing boutique in downtown Stockholm, Sweden, where I grew up. I had worked for them all through high school and had worked in most departments as well as at the cash register. This was how I had paid for all my travels to the US. I had also worked in home care for the elderly as a teenager, but even though I had some work experience, I knew the language barrier was difficult to overcome right at the start and decided to go to the employment center at one of the large universities in Boston. I knew a large university would have a lot of international students and, therefore, may be easier to convince them I was capable of doing work while my English improved. I also thought that by working at a university I would be around more people in my age group. Even though I would be working and they would be students, I was hoping to be able to make friends with some of them. I filled out the paperwork for any administrative job that I qualified for and was then asked to take a typing test.

I was thankful I had taken a class in high school, so I was pretty good at typing. I had never thought that the typing class was going to come to use when I was taking the class. Sometimes when we do things or learn things, we don't understand why until later. It was a scary feeling to be applying for a job in a foreign country. Sometimes they would speak too fast and it was difficult to understand.

After the typing test, I was interviewed by the employment center and sent on for an interview at the engineering school. The interview process went very well, and I was offered a job as the departmental secretary for the biomedical engineering department.

My work duties included having to answer the phone, support the professors, and type all their letters of communication as well as their research papers. One of the professors was very anal in the sense that he would bring his ruler and show me how I had typed something slightly off his preferred margin. Literally by one millimeter! Yes, he was definitely a perfectionist and, of course, a brilliant researcher. Instead of typing in the eleven-millimeter margin, I may have typed in the twelve-millimeter margin. He would almost lose control over himself and make me retype the letter. This was back in the day when we used manual typewriters, and it was sometimes difficult to get the exact margin by millimeter, as I inserted the paper manually. I was typing many research papers almost daily. I had no idea what I was typing, as my English wasn't good enough yet to understand the specific science terms they would use in their research. I specifically remember one research paper that talked a lot about hair and there was this term that stated guinea pig. I asked the professor what kind of pig has long hair, as I thought it was a regular pig and wasn't familiar with the term guinea pig. He laughed so hard that it made me laugh, too, as I figured I must have said something very funny. He understood I really had no idea what the term meant and did his best to explain what kind of an animal a guinea pig was. Language is so easy to understand when you are fluent but can be very difficult when you are learning.

Each day after work, I would go home and watch the youth programming on television. I would watch *The Brady Bunch* and *Happy Days*, as most other TV programming was too difficult to understand. The news was especially hard to understand, as they spoke too quickly and used words I wasn't familiar with. By watching children's and youth programming on TV, my conversational English picked up quickly. I may have sounded like Fonzie on *Happy Days*, but nevertheless, my English improved.

As this was in the early 1980s, computers and computer programming were just becoming a hot topic to study. The university where I worked was one of the first schools that offered online classes. It was a big deal, as the students didn't have to use punch cards to make the programs run. They could type the programming code straight into the computer using a keyboard and monitor. This was quite miraculous back then! The engineering faculty wanted me to transfer my credits from Stockholm's university to the university I was working at and study engineering, as they felt I had a knack for learning programming easily. However, my heart wasn't in engineering, and I thanked them for the advice but decided to transfer to the business school with a minor in management information systems.

Again, I wondered if I should study the sciences, that maybe my father was right; after all, I could be a nurse and it wouldn't take that long. However, I didn't trust I would be able to handle the science classes in a foreign language, so I settled for the business school, as that path seemed easier. Funny how I was consistently choosing a different path than my heart wanted me to be on. However, it taught me many things over the years and has made me who I am today. Nothing is ever a waste. Sometimes, when we go through life, we don't appreciate what we learn and the experiences we gain, as it doesn't seem to matter or make sense to us during that time of our life. I call this the berry-picking part of your life. When you are collecting experiences that will later come to use in your life, you are picking one berry at a time. You will eventually fill your basket with an assortment of berries that will all serve your skills and needs in different ways.

University Studies

I applied to the business school and was accepted as a second-semester sophomore. I carried a dictionary under my arm at all times and would look up all the words I didn't understand. There were times when I would sit through a lecture and barely understand what the teacher was saying. I clearly remember one day in marketing class when the professor gave us an assignment that I wrote down phonetically to the best of my ability to then later decode. When I arrived home to my husband and one of his close friends, I told them what my assignment from class was by reading my phonetic writing on my notes. They look stumped and asked what it was I didn't understand about the assignment. I responded that I had no idea what the words meant that I was saying. I asked them to please explain the meaning of the words I was using so I could understand the assignment. At this point, they burst out laughing, as they understood my dilemma.

I'm sure this is still what it is like for many of our new immigrants who come to our country today. I don't think many people really understand how difficult it is in the beginning when learning a new language and a new culture. If you know someone who has just immigrated, be kind and help them in any way you can. Sometimes it can be difficult to make friends in a new country, especially if there is a language barrier. Jokes were the most difficult to understand for me, as they are often based on puns or knowing the culture or past TV shows, actors, and movies, which when you arrive in a new country, you know nothing about. When everyone was laughing about the joke except for me, it made me feel very isolated. Put yourself in this position; imagine moving to a country that speaks a language you don't understand well or only have a slight knowledge of. It takes time to adjust to a new language and culture. Be kind and patient with immigrants. The immigrants you come in contact with may have been dentists, doctors, or engineers in the country they came from, but now they don't have a license to practice in the US and have to take any job so they can bring in money to pay for food and housing. How would you feel if this was your life experience? Take time to pause and reflect on how this would make you feel to gain a better understanding and empathy for immigrants.

I Thought I Was Going to Die

As my husband graduated from the university, his first job was to manage the first-class lounge at Boston Logan Airport for a major airline. The good part about this job was that we were both eligible to fly stand-by on any of their flights anywhere in the world, which included flights to Sweden, my home country. I was very lucky to be able to fly home during school breaks to see my family so many times.

During a return trip back to the US from Sweden, we started to experience turbulence. We had about two hours to go until we would land at JFK New York. We were on a jumbo jet with two aisles in the plane and the flight attendants were just starting to clear all the trays from dinner. The turbulence kept getting worse and worse, and the flight attendants were giving each other nervous glances as they fought to keep their balance. The plane was bouncing back and forth like a leaf in a windstorm. When I saw the look of concern on my husband's face, I tightened my seat belt, as the turbulence kept worsening. My stomach felt like an empty pit, and my hands were cold and clammy.

All of a sudden, the airplane started falling toward the ground at rapid speed and everything that was loose in the cabin immediately shot up toward the ceiling. The flight attendants, food carts, trays, food, and silverware were flying through the cabin, and the flight attendants were pinned to the cabin ceiling by gravity, as were the large food carts. If you've ever watched one of those airplane disaster movies, you have a good idea of what this scene looked like. It was impossible to control my arms, and they were stretched out straight up above my head. Gravity forced them up, and there was no way to lower my arms. As the plane kept dropping, I was lifted off my seat, and only the seat belt held me in place. The oxygen mask dropped out of the cabin ceiling above me and dangled in front of my face. My arms, being stretched up in the air and without my ability to control them, made it impossible to reach the mask just a few inches in front of my face. I stared at the mask and then glanced out the window. As the plane kept falling, I could see the ocean below me, and I thought, *I didn't think my life was going to end like this! I feel so bad for my parents; they are never going to find us on the bottom of the ocean!*

Shortly after this took place, it was as if we crash-landed into the air. The plane jolted with a simultaneous large cracking sound which made me think it was going to break in half. Everything that was stuck on the cabin ceiling came back down with the same extreme force it had shot up. The large food carts came tumbling down, and one of the flight attendants landed on the headrest in front of us. She spent the rest of the trip lying down resting and looking very pale, and they thought she might have broken her ribs. From what I could see, the large food carts that were closest to us didn't land on anybody but made it back into the aisle with minimal personal damage. The flight attendants who were not injured worked to help passengers and flight attendants who had been injured by the flying trays and glass bottles as well as being catapulted through the cabin. I believe a passenger who had been in the restroom at the time may also have been injured.

During the next two hours of the trip to JFK, you could have heard a pin drop. This was one of my experiences in life when I thought I was going to die. Thinking I was going to die was very different from knowing I was dying. Even though I was an atheist at the time, I prayed to God we would all survive the trip, as I didn't know what else to do.

As we approached JFK and I looked out the window, I could see ambulances and fire trucks lining the runway. I worried the plane was going to break apart during landing, as I had heard the cracking sound during the fall of the plane. The plane did hold together, and I took a deep breath of relief as we hurtled down the runway and came to a stop. As one of my husband's friends was the manager of operations at JFK, I know they kept that plane on the ground for two days to thoroughly inspect it to make sure it was safe to fly. I've learned that airplanes are a lot stronger than I thought, but I still always keep my seat belt on while flying. Again, be grateful for your life every day; you never know when it will end.

Finding Your Path

I bet many of you have had experiences like the one I described above. In these moments, we may realize how fragile life really is, how it can be taken away from us in a split second. We may become more appreciative of our blessings in life. We may be kinder to those we don't get along with and realize the beauty of all that exists. After our initial shock has worn off from a frightening event and we get back to being busy in our lives, we might forget our blessings and our own mortality. Take a moment each day to count your blessings. Would you change the way you live your life if you were told you only have six months left to live? This may sound like it will never happen to you, but working as a physician, I have become more aware of how precious our lives really are. People who appear healthy, happy, and seem to have everything they need in life may be diagnosed with a terminal illness which then takes their life within a year. Think about it. Are you living your life the way you want? Are you following your life path? Are you listening to what your heart is telling you? If not, do something about it!

How do I change my life, you may say. How can I stop working, stop providing for my family? This is not what I mean by changing your life. If you, for example, would like to be an artist, schedule time during your week when you can develop this skill. By making a conscious effort to do something you love or feel motivated to do, you will slowly but surely work toward accomplishing your dreams. You have to start. If you never start, nothing will ever come from it. Once you start, you are moving toward your goal and you will eventually reach it. It's like rolling a snowball down the hill. It gains momentum on the way. I'm working as a physician right now, but I'm setting time aside for myself where I can write, create, and think. I'm not just writing this book; I'm working at the same time. Even if it is late at night or early in the morning, schedule your time. You have to take the initiative to make the change for the change to occur.

Take some time to think about what makes you happy. Does going outside smelling the flowers and the trees make you happy? Does sitting quietly reading a book make you happy? Many things that bring us happiness are free. You don't have to spend money to make yourself happy. Sometimes when I ask people what would make them happy, they reach for things like a vacation on Hawaii, going shopping, buying a new car, etc., which all cost money, but many times it is the small things in life that you will remember for many years. The time you went to get ice cream with a friend and you shared many laughs together can be as joyful or more as an expensive vacation. The time you roasted marshmallows at a campfire with friends or enjoyed a walk in the woods or the beach.

Take time to contemplate life.
Take time to sit still.
Take time to just be you.
You are perfect just the way you are.

As quirky as you may think you are, you are special. Be true to yourself. Sometimes we may have learned to squash our unique self when growing up, as we are constantly told to fit in. Embrace your uniqueness! Many times, we don't appreciate ourselves, but we appreciate others, as many have been taught that thinking of ourselves is selfish. It's not selfish to make sure you are happy and feel content with your life. Stick to being you, just the way you are!

MESSAGE | Find happiness in your heart.

Exercise: What makes you happy? Whatever it is that brings happiness to your heart, find time each day to cultivate this. Even if it is only ten minutes a day in the beginning until you rearrange your schedule to include more time for your special activity, the time you set aside will add up. You have to start in order for a change to occur. Once you start, the intention has been set and your life will start to unfold in a different direction.

9

WISDOM OF CHILDREN

Imaginative Play

I believe children need unstructured time just to explore and use their imagination. Without imagination, nothing would have been invented in the world. If you can't imagine things, how can you develop a new product? How can you set goals for how you would like to live your life if you can't imagine how you would like to live? How can you solve a problem if you have never created a pretend problem to solve while playing? Children learn through imaginative play. They imagine being a firefighter, a doctor, a police officer catching bad guys as well as being imaginative creatures. They imagine being the mom or the dad and emulate their own parents' behavior through imaginative play. It's like practicing being a parent. I see many parents in today's society who think by giving their toddlers worksheets, it will get them ahead. I believe the contrary is true. Let them explore and learn in nature. Let them finger paint, make cookies, and get dirty. Children need to explore to learn about their world and how it works.

Young boys may dress up in girls' clothes and pretend to be a girl or a bride while little girls may dress up in construction clothes or police clothes, which in the past was traditionally more male-dominated jobs in our society. This is how children learn and explore what it "feels like" to be in that role. It allows them to become the person they have dressed up as. This allows the child to explore gender expression and gender identity. If a little boy dresses up in a bride's dress, what is he learning? Maybe he is learning what it's like to feel pretty; maybe this allows him to understand his future bride and wife better. Is it acceptable for him to feel pretty? How does the child feel different dressing up as a bride versus police officer? Does the child act differently when wearing different costumes? Is there a typical behavior he or she is emulating that has been taught by society? Why does the child act tougher when dressed as a police officer versus a bride? How did the child learn this?

As you can see, there are many positive educational experiences that come from just dressing up for a child and pretending to be someone that the child has seen in society. Some parents may not like to see their boys dress up as a bride or a girl dress up as a police officer and will tell the child it is not appropriate and continue to stereotype professions in our society. Maybe the boy dressing up in a bride's dress is going to be a famous designer? Maybe the girl dressing up in police or construction clothes will be a CIA agent? Encourage your child to explore their world without adding in old stereotype messages. If you are one of these parents who believe some dress-up clothes are inappropriate for your child, ask yourself why you think so and where that thought originated. Is this something you decided or something you were told as a child because it wasn't acceptable to your parents? Think about where your thoughts and assumptions stem from.

Many times, I see parents trying to reason with their young children. The children, on the other hand, don't understand what their parents are trying to tell them, as they have not yet developed the higher brain waves needed for reasoning. Bruce H. Lipton discusses the brain waves of young children in chapter four in his book *The Honeymoon Effect: The Science of Creating*

Heaven on Earth. He discusses how adults have five brain wave levels but young children age two to six function on the lower brain wave levels where theta and delta waves dominate. They live in a world of imagination. Thus, when parents try to discipline their children, telling them they are not smart or they don't deserve something, children take this at face value. Many times, these destructive thought patterns follow us into adulthood, making us believe we are lesser.

The Food Co-op

I was also part of a food co-op, as it was difficult and expensive to purchase food from health food stores and there were no big chains like Whole Foods that carried a large assortment of organic produce back then. As the food co-op was about twenty minutes away, I decided to start my own and had about twenty families in the group. The big wholesale food truck would come to our rental house in Huntington Beach, California. They would pull several large pallets of food into my garage. This was the same truck that delivered to the local health food stores all over the region. There was always a lot of excitement about the food truck coming, as everyone had typically been waiting on the food for weeks. We ate a very clean, healthy, and organic diet. At the time, I didn't even have white sugar or white flour in my house.

All the mothers in the group and the older children with ages ranging from about eight to fourteen would help sort everyone's order out while the younger children played on the lawn. Children like to help with grown-up tasks if you allow them. They may make mistakes in the beginning, but if you are patient with them, they are quite capable. It boosts their self-esteem when they can handle adult tasks. Working alongside an adult versus doing a childlike task allows them to feel productive and helpful, as they know they are contributing to the group. Just like rowing the boat for my grandmother as a child allowed me to feel important and useful, which ultimately helped feed the family. Children, of course, are capable at different ages and it's important to not push the child to do things they are not ready to do. If the child is not ready, it will only make his self-esteem worse, as he will feel incapable instead of capable and will wear on your patience as well instead of creating joy.

Early Childhood Education

While the boys were little and I was pregnant with my third child, I attended an early childhood education class at a local college with a wonderful teacher. This was one of the best things I could have done at that time, and I wish all parents would have the opportunity to take a class like this. The book we used was called *Child Behavior from the Gesell Institute of Human Development*. It was a great book and explained the stages children go through each year as well as their fears at particular ages. It was a very helpful book.

We learned many skills on how to control toddler behavior with simple commands. When a toddler was acting up, we learned to redirect the attention and instead of saying "don't do that," which often triggers a young child to do it more, we learned to simply redirect their focus. For example, when you have a group of two- or three-year-olds on tricycles and one of the children repeatedly crashes into the other children, how do you stop them? Just state a fact to have their focus change direction. For this group of children, you would say, "Where are your blinkers?" "Where is your turn signal?" This would then redirect their thoughts from crashing into one another and start pretending to be using turn signals to avoid collisions. Another example would be if a child in the sandbox is throwing sand at the other children. Simply state, "Sand stays on the ground." This simple statement will redirect their actions. This also works well with older children, and I have used this same principle with children as old as twelve when flying through the air pretending to be doing martial arts. Simply state, "Feet stay on the ground," and the behavior will most likely stop.

The Halloween Candy Bowl

When my boys were about five and three, I had put the bowl with the Halloween candy on top of a bookshelf. After a day or two, I noticed the candy level in the bowl was getting lower. Instead of asking the children with the typical blame approach— "Who took candy out of the bowl"—I instead asked, "How did you guys reach the candy on the top shelf?" My oldest child eagerly answered the question with, "It was easy; we just pulled out a chair and climbed up!" Problem solved.

Children are often asked to behave and reason like an adult, and their parents desperately talk to them as if they are teenagers with reasoning capabilities. By learning the developmental stages of your children, you will save yourself a lot of headaches and unnecessary disciplinary actions as well as many premature gray hairs. As much as we would like to think our own children are the most brilliant children in the world, they are still just children. Learn where they are developmentally, and you will have a much easier time disciplining and helping your child grow and develop at their own pace. Nurture them. Listen to the Divine Feminine within you and within them.

The Apple Juice

Children love to be self-sufficient. One day, when I was using the restroom, my child decided to make himself a drink. Upon returning to the kitchen, I discovered he had pulled out one of his tiny plastic cups and put it in the middle of the kitchen floor. He had then opened the refrigerator and grabbed the glass bottle with apple juice. As I entered the kitchen, he was busily pouring the apple juice into his cup on the floor using all his strength holding the bottle with his two little hands. The cup, which was long ago full, was now overflowing onto the kitchen floor, making a large pool of apple juice. He seemed mesmerized by the large lake he was creating.

If you have an active child like this, my advice would be to take life with a grain of salt. Children are constantly learning and exploring and really don't mean to upset you. They are only emulating your behavior, trying to be self-sufficient. Remember this next time your child gets on your nerves. Try to see the humor in the mess that was created. Life isn't really that serious, and you never know what experiences or tragic events could be just around the corner. Enjoy these moments. Take a deep breath and laugh!

The Flour
I went to the garage to put the laundry in the dryer. The boys, now about five and three, were busy at the kitchen counter making cookies with cookie cutters. I could hear them chatting as I tended to the laundry. As I returned to the kitchen, they were both completely covered in flour from head to toe, as they had emptied the whole flour bag and thrown it up in the air. The counter, the chairs they were standing on, their hair, faces, and clothes were all covered in flour! Their eyes were sparkling with excitement as they both smiled and laughed, and I couldn't help but burst out laughing myself. These are the crazy moments you cherish later in life when you realize the comedy of it all. As difficult and tiring as some of these situations were, I never regret having made the sacrifice to live on one income in order

to stay home and raise my children. There are just too many funny memories like these that were created during this time which will always stay with me. Not all women want to stay at home and raise their children, and I truly respect that. However, I wish our society would be more supportive to allow women a choice and not make it so difficult to live on one income, which for many families is not even an option.

Dressing

My daughter was an expert at being a stubborn two-year-old when it came to dressing herself. Those of you who have had or have children this age can probably relate to the stubbornness of two-year-olds. One of her favorite outfits was a pretty white lace dress with her white winter snow boots. She would wear this outfit regardless of what the activity or weather was. There were times I would receive stares from people in the grocery store as if to say, "Why are you letting your child go out this way?" Does it matter that your child is not wearing a perfect outfit? No, not really. Save the battle for something that does matter, and let them get their way at times with the small stuff that doesn't matter. It will save you a lot of gray hairs.

Stand Your Ground

When my children were about nine, seven, and four and we lived in the middle of Long Island, New York, they were blessed by having friends right next door whom they played with every day. However, the parents were much stricter in their childrearing than I was, and I'm sure they at times must have thought I was a European hippie. I remember one time the mother was not pleased with my actions when I had allowed my children a small amount of ice cream before dinner. Now her children wanted ice cream before dinner, and it was pretty much my fault.

Don't let other people suppress your thoughts or actions or tell you what you should think or do, as this will then manifest and rule your subconscious. When your child's blood sugar is low and you are trying to keep them going until dinner, ask yourself, *If this were my fourth child instead of my first child asking me if they could have some ice cream, would I even care?*

Homeschooling

We decided to homeschool our children when they were young, as we wanted to allow them more time to play and gear their education toward their interests. My sister-in-law was a big influence on me regarding the choice to homeschool, and upon her recommendation, I went to the library and borrowed ten to fifteen books to understand what it was all about. I read all the books John Holt had written and anything else I could get my hands on, including *Dumbing Us Down* by John Taylor Gatto.

Children all learn very differently. Some children are "busy learners" and not very good at sitting still when learning and need to move around and explore, or what we call kinesthetic learners. My mother-in-law and my sister-in-law were both teachers as well, so I had plenty of help in figuring out what and how to teach. We were part of many different large home-schooling groups, and the kids had plenty of opportunities to socialize with other children their own age.

Children are all born with their own personalities, and we all arrive into the world being our unique selves. As we ended up homeschooling our children past the lower-school grades due to them later working in the professional performing arts scene, it made me realize how difficult it must be for teachers in school. What a challenge to teach so many kids. I only taught my own three children using the same curriculum, and they all had a different learning style and grasped concepts at different ages.

One child would be ready for high-level math two years before another child, but the other child would be two years ahead in English. As they grew older and entered into their junior high school years, their learning styles and intellect evened out.

All you teachers out there, you have my blessings!

Activities

When my oldest son was nine years old, he was notorious for looking at the sky instead of watching his teammates when playing soccer. One day, on our way home from a soccer game, I asked him what he was doing on the field and why he wasn't paying attention to the soccer game. His response was, "I'm singing!" Well, that confirmed he was not really enjoying soccer. Both my husband and I had played soccer when we were young, so we assumed our son would enjoy it, too. We took him out of soccer and enrolled him in a children's theater group, which he loved.

Pay attention to your children. Are they enjoying the activity, or are you trying to make them do something you yourself enjoyed as a child? What makes them tick? You are their advocate. Help your children feel confident and smart. You must boost your child's ego—not your own.

Listen to Your Heart

As the kids were growing up, I focused on teaching them one thing: to follow their heart. There were times when they would be worried about their future, career choices, which college they would need to attend in order to succeed in life. I always told them I really didn't care which school they went to, nor what job title they would have as an adult. I told them we are all here to fulfill our own life's journey. "Only you know what makes your heart happy. Only you are in charge of your life," I would tell them.

If you listen to your heart and do what it tells you, it will help fulfill your dreams. As a result, other people sense your peace and happiness, which can then contribute to your success. If you have a love for bicycles and want to fix bicycles, then people will know about you because your love will be infectious. They will sense your love and passion and will be drawn toward you. I always told my kids that I didn't care if they grew up and became milk bottle cap collectors. If they really loved milk bottle caps, they would be famous for their collection and knowledge. In the end, it is all about the passion in your heart.

Berry-picking

Many times, when my children would experience a "tizzy" about not yet knowing what to do with their lives, I would tell them to enjoy life and not to worry. "You are in the 'berry-picking' part of your life," I would tell them. Imagine you are out in a beautiful field carrying a little basket; the sun is shining, and it's a perfect day. The field is filled with different kinds of berries. Blueberries, raspberries, strawberries, blackberries, and any other berry you can imagine. I would tell them, "You are in this field right now; you are to pick and taste as many berries as you can. By tasting all the different berries, you will find the ones you like the most." Enjoy the fact that you don't know what to do. At this stage in life, you have a chance to learn and taste different things, and by doing so, you will find what resonates in your heart and with your destiny.

Once you have picked a lot of berries and your basket is full, you are ready to make jam. This jam that you make is from all the life experiences you have collected along the way. All the berries together are creating a new life jam. It is all the berries together that give you new opportunities and adventures, allowing your soul to grow.

Listen to your heart, and your path will unfold. No search is needed. Just listen. Once my children found what they were passionate about, I would tell them, "Flap your wings! I know you can fly."

The Angel

When my oldest child was two years old and I was pregnant with my second child, I was getting him ready to go to the playground. All of a sudden, he started staring at the corner of the ceiling. After he had been staring for a while, I asked him what he was looking at. He said, "There is an angel in the corner of the ceiling." I was surprised at his response, as we had never talked about angels. I asked him what the angel was doing. He responded with, "She is watching us." After I finished dressing him, I asked, "What is the angel doing now?" He looked up again at the corner of the ceiling and simply stated, "Oh, she is gone now."

As I was a complete atheist at the time and didn't believe in anything I couldn't verify, I brushed off the incidence as imaginary play. Now that many years have passed and my children are adults, I have heard similar stories from other parents where their young children have stated there were angels around them and that they could see them. Are children more connected to the Divine Universe? Are we allowing them to be spiritual, or do we tend to tell them there is nothing there and they are wrong because we aren't able to see what they see? Think about how you treat these moments. Was your own spirituality suppressed in childhood?

Past Lives

In other cultures, it is believed that children remember their previous lives and can be asked questions about it when they are young. My personal belief is that children are much more connected spiritually both to previous lives as well as being able to see things in their current lives that most of us adults can't. You may have been able to see things as a child but have learned to suppress these capabilities growing up as you tried to adjust and behave how is socially acceptable in our society.

Are we just more tuned in as children and then lose this ability as we grow older and become more grounded in what we believe to be reality? Our expressions are usually discounted as imaginary when we are children. There have been studies done on children who have been able to tell stories about their past lives, and Dr. Ian Stevenson has written many books on this topic. Have you had experiences like this in your own life but have never been brave enough to share with anyone else in fear of being thought of as crazy?

Many people have spiritual gifts but are afraid of sharing them even with their loved ones for fear they will be discounted in some way. Maybe you could see spirits as a child or experienced other supernatural encounters and your parents suppressed this by telling you it was your imagination.

When I was around nine or ten years old and walking to school with my friend, I told her I knew I'd been a witch in a previous life. I was really a healer, but they were called witches back then. I told her I was burned at the stake but I was some-how dead before they burned me. My friend looked at me and said, "You are crazy! That is scary! Why do you think that?" I told her I didn't really know but that I had always thought so.

Do you have memories from previous lives? Do you remember who you were maybe many hundreds of years ago? The inter-esting part of this is when a medical medium read me over the phone during this past year, she suddenly exclaimed, "You were a witch long ago. You were a healer; they were called witches then. You were burned at the stake, but you were already dead when they burned you because witches back then knew how to hold their breath and die before being burned." Was this a coincidence? How could that be? Do our past lives exist in our energy grid that we carry with us? What were the chances this woman would say this not knowing anything about me?

If you think about your own life, there are probably many instances that you have had similar experiences but brushed them off as coincidental. Take notice next time something like this happens in your life; is it really a coincidence?

When I was a little girl, there was a news clip on TV about the island of Molokai and the leprosy patients that lived there. I looked at my dad and said, "I used to be one of those nuns taking care of the sick people." My dad just smiled, as I'm sure he thought it was my imagination. Even though my dad brushed it off, this knowledge has always stayed with me in my heart. About a year ago, I met a woman who reads people and discovers their past lives. I went to her home, and she took my hand and closed her eyes. She said, "Your last life was on the island of Molokai; you were a nun there and took care of the people with leprosy."

MESSAGE | Don't suppress your children's voices. Listen to them. Maybe you were given a particular child in this life to help *you* see the world through a different lens.

Exercise: If you have children of your own or have nieces and nephews or maybe younger siblings, think about how you treat them. Are they telling you things you are uncomfortable with? Are they trying to teach *you* something? Pay attention to the children around you; they may be bringing *you* messages.

10

JUST DO IT

The Kitten

As we arrived at the boys' martial arts class one afternoon in 1997, another child's father had brought a young kitten. It was only a few days old, and they had rescued it from their barn where the kitten had gotten trapped between cinder blocks. They had searched for the mother but hadn't been able to locate her. The family was unable to keep the kitten due to one of his children being severely allergic, so he had brought it with him in hopes one of the families in the school would adopt her. My daughter, who was five years old at the time, wanted to hold the kitten right away and begged me to let us keep her. The father handed my daughter the kitten, and she hugged it tightly and knew to be careful; she was a natural.

We already had two large dogs, a large black long-haired dog with pointy ears and long nose that we had named Natasha and another large black long-haired dog that sort of looked like a black golden retriever that we had named Mozart. We really didn't need any more animals. I watched my daughter holding and kissing the little kitten the entire time her brothers were in class, and I already knew this little one was meant to go home with us.

As we drove home from martial arts with the kitten in my oldest son's lap, we were discussing the best way to introduce her to my husband. We were all a little nervous about how he would react, as we knew he loved dogs but not so much cats, at least not yet! As we approached our house in the cul-de-sac, we were surprised to see his car already parked on the driveway. Though he never lost his temper, we were still afraid that he would be upset with us. As we pulled into the driveway, my husband greeted us at the car window where my son was sitting, holding the kitten in his lap.

"What is it that you have in your lap, son?" he asked.

My oldest son smiled and stated proudly, "A kitten!"

My husband cleared his throat and wasn't sure how to respond, and it was awkwardly quiet for a moment.

My mind said, *Oh shoot, he is not too pleased!* Even though I could tell he didn't approve of my actions at the time, the kitten grew on him, and he fell in love with it within a week.

Life is meant to be enjoyed. Sometimes you have to bring spontaneity into your life in order to create excitement. If you never do things out of the ordinary, then your life will become dull. Fill your life with adventures and excitement when you can.

The Beagle

A few months before our move back to California, our dog Mozart, who was only three years old, experienced kidney failure and passed away. Natasha, our other dog, seemed to miss her friend, but as we were only months away from moving back to California where the backyards are typically smaller than the one we had in New York, we decided to not get another dog at that time.

Shortly after our move back to California in May of 1998, the children and I went to the pet store to get dog food and saw an adorable, spunky blue tick beagle. *Perfect*, we all thought. She was just the right size and would be a good companion for our dog, Natasha. We decided to get her, and the kids were ecstatic as we left the store with the puppy. I was a bit concerned about how I was going to tell my husband that we had just gotten a dog without including him in the decision-making process. But we all felt this was the right dog, and my husband happened to be away on business travels. It was also my fortieth birthday that weekend.

My mother-in-law would always tell me, "If you want something, just get it! Don't ask! If you ask, they will say no," meaning her own husband as well as her son (my husband). Knowing this and remembering that my husband was raised by my mother-in-law, I took my chance. I put a note on the front door for my husband's return that said, "Thank you for the birthday present!"

When my husband returned home from his travels, he came into the living room cautiously and wondered what I possibly could have done that had provoked me to put up such a note. As he entered the kitchen and discovered the little beagle, he immediately fell in love and thought it was a good idea, as it was a smaller dog and would make a good companion for the large dog. We all took a deep breath and were happy he liked the puppy.

If you never take action, nothing will ever happen. Sometimes you have to take risks and leap into the unknown so you don't miss out on new experiences and adventures that will take you down a new path in life.

The Lhasapoo

Two weeks later, the kids and I returned to the pet store to get more dog food. As we entered the store, the children ran over to the cages where the puppies and kittens were. They immediately discovered a very cute little tan-colored dog the size of a Beanie Baby. The dog literally looked like a toy! It was a Lhasapoo, a cross between a Lhasa Apso and a poodle. My middle child fell absolutely in love with this dog, and he had always been afraid of animals, even our own dogs, since he'd been a baby. When we had brought home the big black dogs as puppies, he was so afraid he would sometimes stand on the kitchen benches before he got used to them. This was a breakthrough! I was so excited he actually wanted this dog. The kids begged me to call their father to ask if we could please get this little dog.

I called my husband on my cell phone from the pet store. My children had formed a semi-circle in front of me and were anxiously waiting for their father to pick up the phone. My middle child wiped the tears off his face and looked at me with his glossy eyes, waiting to hear his father's response. The other two children looked up at me, wide-eyed in anticipation.

As I described to my husband what was going on, he said, "Whatever you do, *don't get another dog!*"

I looked at the children and kept agreeing with my husband on the phone before I hung up.

The children were all looking at me with their starry and hopeful eyes, and they all said in unison, "What did he say?"

I looked at them and said, "He said, *get it!*"

The kids went wild and ran over to claim the little dog as theirs, whom they named Elvis.

When we got home, I tried to figure out how to present this purchase to my husband. I felt bad that I had stepped out of line and gone against his wishes, but I also knew this would be the dog that would help my son overcome his fear of animals.

My niece was visiting, as she was traveling through the area on business. I explained to her what was going on, and we quickly came up with a plan, as she felt the same about the dog as I did and supported my decision. We all went outside in the backyard, which pretty much consisted of a cemented patio around a pool with a picnic table and umbrella at one end of the yard. As my husband returned home from work, he found us outside, and we immediately asked if he wanted a cold beer.

He laughed and said, "Hmmm, such good and welcoming treatment. What are you guys up to?" At this point, he took a step backward just as the little dog Elvis ran behind him.

We all gasped and exclaimed, *"Watch out! Don't step on him,"* at which point my husband looked both surprised and worried and exclaimed, "Step on what?" He turned around and saw little Elvis and looked at me straight in the eye and said, *"You didn't!"* He then sat on a chair at the table almost as if in shock. At this point, I wasn't sure how he was going to react, and I wondered if I had gone too far this time. *I shouldn't have done this*, I thought. As he sat at the picnic table, I put little Elvis on his chest. As he was petting the tiny dog, he of course immediately fell in love with him and said, "Well, it's a good thing I'm a sucker for animals!" After all, he had been raised with several golden retrievers as well as sheep and chickens in a suburban home. His mother was a schoolteacher and had learned to do what she needed to do in life, as when she asked for permission, the answer would undoubtedly be no. In a way, he thrived on these surprises but always tried to be the responsible dad he had been taught to be.

Little Elvis did wonders for my son who was afraid of animals, and the dog became his best friend. There was also an unusually strong bond between my husband and Elvis.

Trust your intuition. Just do it!

Another Earthquake

One night in the spring of 1999, a year after we had moved back to California from New York, my husband was away on business travels and all the kids had laid down on our bed to read stories. They had just fallen asleep, and as a parent, I treasured these moments. As I was admiring the closeness of my children and watching them all piled up next to each other on our bed, like three little angels, the house started to shake violently. It was a big one! A 7.2-magnitude earthquake. The doors were swinging from side to side, and it felt like a large train was going through my house or a helicopter landing on my roof. I struggled to get to my feet as I yelled at the top of my lungs for the kids to wake up and take shelter. The children were in a deep sleep already, and none of them heard me. I kept yelling as loud as I could, but the rumble from the quake made such a large noise that my voice was drowned out by the sound. I struggled to keep my balance and get to the doorway, which at the time was considered the safest spot in the event of an earthquake. There was no way I could even try to grab the children, as the shaking was so violent. My adrenalin was rushing through my veins, as I worried the ceiling would start to cave in and harm my children. If I got to safety, I would at least be able to rescue them should they get harmed in any way. The house kept shaking, and I kept yelling for them to wake up. They finally heard me and woke just as I reached the doorway. The earthquake started to calm down, though the doors were still swinging from side to side.

They all sat straight up in bed, and the oldest child exclaimed, "Mom, there is an earthquake!"

At this point, I started laughing and said, "Yes, there is an earthquake!" I was so happy we were all okay, and the kids all ran to the window of our bedroom, which was on the second floor of our house overlooking the cement patio and pool.

They all yelled, "Mom, the pool overflowed!"

We ran downstairs, as we could hear the motor of the pool making loud noises. We discovered that so much of the pool had overflowed the water level was below the water intake for the pool motor. The water had literally levitated out of the pool. As we came into the kitchen to get through the family room and out to the pool, we noticed the entire family room had one to two inches of pool water covering the floor. The water had been pushed through the bottom of the closed sliding door. I turned off the pool motor, and the kids helped sweep the water out to the patio with brooms.

It was a long night, and we used every towel we owned to dry the floor.

Never take anything for granted. Natural disasters and accidents can happen at any time. Enjoy every moment of your life!

Moving in with Friends

The kids were either performing or in rehearsal from September 1998 to New Year's of the following year, 1999, except for one week! It was a crazy year, and I enjoyed it so much, as I had finally recovered enough to be able to take the kids where they needed to be without always feeling faint and weak. The fight to stay alive had definitely paid off.

As you go through life, there are times when the wind will blow hard and there will be torrential downpours, but the sun always comes out in the end. If you are going through a tough time now, don't give up. Eventually, things will get better. Nothing lasts forever.

My eldest child was a solo child singer in a professional holiday production that would put on around eighty shows between Thanksgiving and Christmas. This meant on a day that he was performing, he would sing in three shows and then have two days off. In this show, the adults were double cast and the children triple cast. The younger two children were also performing in the show, and there were many late nights. As a result, we had decided to homeschool through the school district that year, as it would have been impossible to stay on a regular school schedule with an early morning wake-up after a long night performing.

In May of 1999, my husband got word that we were to be moved again, and we had a choice of moving to Hawaii or San Francisco. As the kids were deep into the performing arts, we chose San Francisco to give the kids more opportunities to excel and follow their passions. As my oldest son had already signed a contract to perform in the upcoming season's holiday production for the same show he had performed in the year prior, we moved into our house in East Bay San Francisco over the Halloween weekend. We unpacked and quickly set up the house for my husband and left him in charge of the four cats as we returned down to Orange County for rehearsals with the three dogs.

As we no longer owned the house in Orange County, we moved in with our best friends. This was the friend who had showed up on my doorstep when I was recovering, sitting in the rocking chair. We had a lot of fun, and as my friend would say, "One dad, two moms, three dogs, four cats, and five children." We had left our four cats in San Francisco with my husband, but they also had four cats, which allowed this funny rhyme to come about. It was interesting to see how much easier everything was with two moms. One of us would always be around for the kids while the other could run errands and pick things up at the grocery store. We always joked about what had happened to our society. This must have been what it was like even just a hundred years ago. Everything was so much easier. Shared housework, shared cooking, shared errands, shared child-watching.

We have isolated ourselves in our own society, which we ourselves created. Why don't we live like this anymore? Maybe we should build large houses with a large community kitchen and family room where two to three families who have been carefully matched live together, with each family having their own section of the house that can be closed off as needed. A sort of community living where parents can take turns helping with cooking, homework, and babysitting. Someone is always around, providing support and help for each other. This could also be done for the elderly population, where several older self-sufficient people shared a common area and looked out for one another as well as providing socialization and stimulation instead of being isolated living on their own. They, too, could help one another with errands and cooking.

Just Do It

If you want something, you have to take action. What I did may not have been the best option for everyone else. If our relationship had been different, I would most likely have consulted my husband before adding all those animals. Knowing how he had grown up and his own mother telling me to "just do it" made my life a little different. However, whenever you want to accomplish something, listen to your heart and just start. If you don't start, nothing will come from it. You have to take action and initiate change for it to occur. Sometimes, we need to take chances to make things happen and change our paths. The worst thing that can happen is that you fall and will have to get back up and start again. By initiating change and starting, you are creating the path you would like to walk on.

Imagine yourself in the woods. There are lots of branches in the way, but you have an ax and a saw, and you start cutting down the branches one by one that block your way. You are creating a new path. Unlock your heart and let the divine existence of all that is into your heart. Everything you want already exists within you ready to materialize in the physical world. Your thoughts create your existence. Maybe you are more in tune with the divine existence of all that is than you think! You need to take action in order for things to materialize in the physical world.

MESSAGE | Just do it!

Exercise: Are you spontaneous? If not, create some spontaneity in your life. Do something you usually wouldn't do. If you never allow yourself to have fun on a work night, then allow yourself to do something fun on these nights to break up the monotony in your life. Just do it!

11

THE MESSAGES

My Spiritual Earth Guide

After I had my out-of-body experiences, my mother-in-law brought me the book *Life after Life* by Raymond Moody. She was my earth guide to spirituality. This book helped me understand what was going on in my life, and she brought me many books on the topic throughout the next couple of years. As the years passed, we had many conversations about life, and she helped me find my spiritual path. Without her guidance, my spirituality would not have unfolded the way it has.

I believe we are given people to guide us through life if we just pay attention. We all have guides, both spiritual and earthly, that help us through life. Open your eyes, and you will find them. It may be a close friend or someone you don't know very well who all of a sudden steps forward. It may be a stranger or coworker. The point is, don't judge people. Some of the people you are judging at a distance may be people who you are supposed to connect with and learn something from, as unlikely as it may seem at the moment. Maybe the people you don't really like are teaching you a lesson. When someone is nudging you in a good or bad way, they may be trying to make you realize you need to make a change or learn something new. There may be a lesson you are supposed to learn. We are all connected.

The Messages

In July 2004, at age 46, exactly twelve years since my first NDE in the ER, I felt as though I had finally healed physically, emotionally, and spiritually. I sat down at my computer in the living room to search for an online program in health that I could start. My children were now eighteen, fifteen, and twelve, and it was time to start thinking about what I wanted to do when I returned to the workforce. As I had always been interested in medicine, I searched for anything that had to do with health and healing. I stumbled across naturopathic medicine and was immediately drawn to the field. However, it was a real medical school, and though I knew I had always wanted to become a doctor, it didn't seem realistic. *Going to medical school at my age, that is a lot of work, and I probably wouldn't even get accepted,* I thought. My intellect told me the stakes were too high both in terms of time and money and no guarantee I would even get accepted into a program like that at my age. Even if I managed to get accepted, there was no guarantee I would graduate. I let go of the thought and figured something else would come up.

I stood from my computer and started to walk toward the kitchen. Suddenly, I became aware of a spirit guide who was communicating with me. As I had become accustomed to receiving messages by now, I knew to listen carefully. I stopped in the middle of the room and stared up into the ceiling, wondering if I would be able to see the spirit guide. I couldn't see anything, but I could sense a presence and hear the spirit guide giving me messages telepathically. The spirit guide gave me four messages:

1. You have to become a naturopathic doctor.
2. You are to integrate East and West.
3. You will bring messages and healing to the people.
4. You will write two books—no, wait—three.

*I understood immediately that I needed to go to medical school. I
also understood the message about integrating East and West and
interpreted that as combining old and new treatment modalities.
In a sense, that is what naturopathic medicine is about. I asked the
spirit guide what the message about bringing messages to the people
meant and what I was supposed to write about, as I had never
thought of myself as an author. The spirit guide continued.*

*You need to go to medical school and become a doctor first.
When the time is right, we will tell you the next steps.
You will know later what the books and messages are about.*

I understood from the message that I was to become a doctor
first, as that was the base for my future path and destiny in life.
It was clear that my work was to be divided between working
as a physician, healer, author, and something else that was to be
revealed later as my path unfolded. The message was so strong
and direct that I enrolled in medical school prerequisite classes
within a week. I trusted the message instinctively. The spirit
world had shown me for the past twelve years to learn to trust
in the messages I was receiving. This was something I had to
do. It was divine fate. This time, there was no thinking if I was
crazy even though parts of the message didn't make sense at
the time. I had always known I was here to help people heal. I
knew the time had come when I needed to make that leap, as
crazy as this sounded to the intellectual side of my brain.

I picked up the phone and called my best friend to tell her
what was happening. I told her, "I'm healed! I did it! I'm going
to medical school!" She was, of course, very excited for me and
glad to hear I had made progress in putting all the pieces together
from the last twelve years. I figured she must think I was crazy

to contemplate going to medical school at my age, but she didn't say anything and was very supportive. We all have spirit guides, and we need to train ourselves to listen to their messages.

Prerequisites for Med School

I was very proud and excited as I walked across the campus on the first day of class. I started with biology, as I thought that would be easier compared to chemistry. I wasn't able to start with freshman biology but had to take the advanced placement high school biology first, as I didn't have that prerequisite class. It had been many years since I had been in school and studied, and I was nervous about being able to keep up with the younger population.

After a few weeks in school, I had settled in. It was a very different college experience compared to when I went in the early 1980s. The pace was a lot faster, as the teacher used PowerPoints and didn't have to write on the blackboard. My biology teacher kept telling us there was so much new material in the science classes that they had to teach at hyper speed. The length of time they had to teach the course was the same as it had been many years ago. They were expected to cover all the material in one semester per class, but he told us he was hoping that would change and be split up into three biology classes instead of two.

After completing this first class, I had adapted to the new type of school and speed. I was thinking about how stressed the undergraduate student today must be with all the classes moving at such a fast pace. What had happened to the good old days when you could stare out the window while the teacher wrote on the board? Now there were no breaks, and it took my constant concentration to follow along. I wondered if this had contributed to the rise in ADD.

For the next few years, I took one class at a time. After completing high school biology and chemistry, I moved on to parts one and two in biology, chemistry, and organic chemistry as well as physics and math. I signed up for one class per semester, as I was busy running my own business and still helping my kids get through high school. There were days when I wouldn't be able to get to my homework during the day. Exhausted, I would go to bed at 10:00 p.m. and then wake at 4:00 a.m. to do homework until 7:00 a.m. and then leave for class by 7:30 a.m. I would be in class all morning, then come home and eat lunch and then immediately jump in the car to drive my kids to the city for their classes. Sometimes, I would do my homework in the car while waiting for my kids, who were either in class, rehearsing, or performing. It was definitely a busy couple of years juggling family, school, and work, but I kept my focus on my path and moved forward at a steady pace. Because I took the initiative to start, it led me down a new path, and one class led to another.

Don't be afraid to make changes in your life; start by taking a step in a new direction. It doesn't matter how big or small the step is; just the fact that you are taking a step is what will create change.

Med School Application

It was early spring in 2010, and the day had arrived when I started the application process to apply to medical school. I was so excited about the possibility of getting accepted and carefully reviewed each of the schools online to learn more about them. I decided to apply to a school in Seattle, Washington, and one in Phoenix, Arizona. I was attracted to Seattle, as it was a city on the coast and I had always lived close to water. I was a little bit worried about applying to the school in Phoenix, as it was located in the desert, but nevertheless, I was drawn to this school. I requested the application packet from both schools, and two big packets of information arrived in the mail. The first steps in the process of applying to medical school involved ensuring I was academically ready and requesting transcripts from previous schools attended as well as ensuring I had completed all the prerequisite classes before applying. The second step was to write an application letter answering several questions each requiring a certain number of words.

The first question on the application asked about my accomplishments. I felt this question was pretty easy, as I had a lot of life experience to draw on. I wrote about my work accomplishments after college, which consisted of being a programmer and systems analyst for a major corporation as well as starting and running my own e-commerce business and then returning to work as a sales representative and sales manager for a biotech company. I felt good about my first answer and moved on to the second question, which asked about how I had dealt with a challenge during work. I felt this was a character type of question, and I thought about instances that I could talk about. I decided to describe a situation where I had changed the behavior of someone by teaching how their behavior and word choices affected those around them. I introduced a person to Dr. Masaru Emoto's work on water, pointing out how different water crystals form depending on what words and music the water is exposed to. When the water was exposed to beautiful classical music, it formed a beautiful crystal, but after being exposed to music that used profanity, it formed ugly images. There are also examples on YouTube where sand makes different formations based on frequencies and sounds.

I kept thinking, *Am I answering these questions the way they want me to answer them? Are they going to like my answers? What is the younger age group giving as their answer to these questions? Are my answers going to look like they are coming from an old person?* I decided to stop worrying about the other applicants and only worry about my own answers. *How would I guide my own children in this process?* I thought. *I would tell them to listen to their hearts!* To compete with the other unknown applicants in my brain didn't serve me any good, and I needed to focus on my answers and what *my* life had taught *me*. *Listen to your heart*, I told myself. I moved on to the next question.

The third question on the application asked me about personal accomplishments, and I wrote about how I was proud of homeschooling our three children. Except for basic reading, writing, and math, I embraced an "un-schooling" curriculum and relied heavily on the interests of each child. All three children were gifted in the performing arts, which led to a heavy performance schedule. They had each performed around two hundred professionally staged shows, and I had been the driver and chaperone for almost all these shows.

The fourth question asked about any previous studies related to health, and I wrote about my experience studying nutrition in the late 1980s.

I was now done with the easy background type of questions, and I was moving on to the more in-depth questions of why I wanted to go to medical school in the first place. *Yeah, what made me consider applying to medical school in my fifties after entering menopause? I better have a good answer to these questions*, I thought. I couldn't exactly tell them the spirit world told me I needed to become a doctor! How was I supposed to convince them on paper that I was at least worth an interview? If I could land an interview, I felt I would have a better chance being accepted, as I looked younger than my age. *Did I complete all the prerequisite classes for no reason? I better get accepted*, I thought.

Stick with it, and never give up on your dreams.

I moved on and read the next question, which asked me why I wanted to become a naturopathic physician as well as some other questions. I took a deep breath. How could I answer this question using only three hundred words max? I started writing about how I had always wanted to become a doctor for as long as I could remember. I talked about my father, who was an MD and family practitioner, and my mother, who had returned to work as a hospital floor administrator when I was twelve and how one of my brothers had become a surgeon. I had grown up surrounded by medicine but had never listened to my heart. I wrote about my NDEs and struggles with health and how it had changed the way I viewed medicine and life itself. After rewriting this section several times, I hit three hundred words exactly. I was finally satisfied with my answers, decided it was now in the hands of the Divine Universe, and mailed my applications.

After much waiting, I received a letter from the school in Washington as well as the one in Arizona stating that I had been invited to a personal interview at both schools. I was ecstatic. Maybe this was possible after all. *Never give up on your dreams,* I thought.

Medical School Interview

I scheduled a flight to Phoenix for my interview and a room at a hotel close to the location of the school in Tempe. My eighteen-year-old daughter accompanied me on the trip, and even though it was November and Phoenix was quite cold, I was determined to rent a convertible car, as I felt I had to do something I usually wouldn't do to celebrate the fact that I had landed an interview. As we drove around with the top down on the convertible, the people in Phoenix must have thought we were crazy, as it was cold and they were bundled up. We received many blank stares from nearby drivers, but it was just so exciting to be going for an interview that the cold winds blowing in our faces didn't seem to bother us. I wanted to shout out to the world that I was there for an interview. I felt so excited and alive! I was following my heart, dream, and the message I had received years prior from the spirit world.

As I arrived on campus, I was directed to the administrative building and took the elevator up to the assigned floor. My stomach had butterflies, and I hadn't been able to eat much that morning, as I was nervous about the interview and how I was going to be perceived as being older than most other applicants. Upon exiting the elevator, I was directed to the room where the applicants were gathering for their interview. Several tables were set up in a big room in a horseshoe formation. There were probably around thirty nervous-looking applicants of all ages and ethnicities in the room. There was a table with a breakfast buffet, and we all had some breakfast and made small talk with one another as we anxiously waited on instructions. It was time to take a seat, and the staff members welcomed us. We were each given our interview time of the day and would take turns leaving the group to attend our interview.

After a short welcome, we were divided into groups for an icebreaker activity. We were then taken on a tour of the school including the state-of-the-art cadaver lab, where some students were busy working, studying for an exam and locating various nerves, muscle groups, and organs. It was an eerie feeling, standing in a room with seven cadavers, as this was something I had never experienced before. The cadavers had all been persevered in formaldehyde, which has a tendency to smell very strong, but as it was a state-of-the-art lab and the ventilation was very good, it didn't smell at all. We were all wide-eyed but worked hard to keep cool.

Different games and evaluations took place during the day, and it was finally my turn to go to the room where the interview would take place. As I entered, there were three people present that were to ask me questions and evaluate me to see if I was a candidate for medical school. It was nerve-wracking! I had to convince them I was a good candidate despite my age. This was the day I had been waiting for; had I done all that work in vain?

I introduced myself and took my seat. They fired one question after another about why I would want to enter medical school and become a doctor as well as my work ethics and many other questions. Did I have the stamina, intellect, and personality to go through a rigorous program, and did I understand how much work was involved and the fact that if I didn't pass exams I would flunk out? Did I understand there were no guarantees I would make it through the program, and was I willing to take this risk leaving my current well-paying job behind and moving to another state? A lot was at stake. The interview took about one hour and went very well, and I was now more determined than ever that I wanted to be accepted into the program. I understood it was probably going to be a lot of work and definitely harder than undergraduate classes, but I really had no idea how hard a program like that was. After an entire day of evaluations, interviews, and tours of the school, I returned to the hotel and my daughter. I was so excited and told her about everything I had experienced during the day. She was very excited for me and told me I would for sure get accepted. How she could be so sure? I didn't know.

We flew back to the Bay Area, San Francisco, the next morning.

A few weeks went by, and the time had come for the interview at the school in Seattle. I flew in late in the evening after work and stayed at a hotel downtown. The next morning, I drove out to the campus for the interview. The school was located on beautiful grounds and had been used as a Catholic seminary in the past. This interview was set up differently from the school in Arizona, and I was interviewed by a staff member for about an hour and then given a tour of the school. I was the only candidate interviewed in this time slot. I was again impressed and didn't know which school I wanted to attend more should I be accepted.

In the afternoon, I drove downtown to tour their clinic. I was introduced to the students and the doctor that was running a shift and was shown around the clinic. As the day came to an end, I had given it my best and hoped I would at least get admitted to one of the schools. If I didn't get admitted to either of the two, I could always apply to other schools.

I was now more determined than ever. How had the spirit guide that had given me the message years ago known? Was my life planned? I felt so at home in the clinics and the environment of medicine and couldn't wait for the day I would find out if I had been accepted.

Acceptance

A few months went by, and I received a call from the school in Arizona while I was at work. I had been accepted into the program! I was so excited I had tears of happiness rolling down my cheeks. I needed to tell my friend at work and made my way over to her cube. I was so excited I was afraid I would lose it and start crying out loud. I wiped my tears off my face as my friend gave me a hug. She was so happy for me. I then received the formal letter of acceptance in the mail, and the same scenario took place with the school in Washington. I couldn't believe it! The past few years had been preparation work for this day, and it was happening! I was so excited and could barely contain myself! I just wanted to scream out, *"I'm going to medical school! Never give up on your dreams!"*

I let both schools know I was interested in attending, but I needed to decide which to attend. Every night when I went to bed, I would meditate on which school was right for me. I was really drawn to Arizona and kept getting the message from a spirit guide that the people I needed to meet and work with in the future were all in Arizona. However, Seattle was on the coast, and I had always lived by a body of water. Why was I getting a message to go to Arizona? It was difficult to know the right decision. Was I imagining the messages from the spirit world? Why wasn't this as clear as the message about going to medical school? Each time I decided I wanted to go to the school in Washington, I would wake each night doubting this was the right decision, and my spirit guide would tell me I needed to go to Arizona. This would go on for about two weeks. Then I would decide that Arizona was the right decision, and I would sleep through the night for the next two weeks. Eventually, after months of this, I decided the Universe was trying to tell me to go to Arizona. After all, how many times did I have to keep being woken up at night to receive the same message? It was time to trust the messages and guidance I was receiving. Why was I so hesitant to trust the messages now when I had blindly trusted the messages before? My left brain of reasoning kept getting in my way. I wanted proof.

We all receive guidance from the spirit world; it's just a matter of listening, paying attention, and trusting those messages. Even though I had an NDE and was used to experiencing many clairvoyant moments, I still had a difficult time trusting that which I could not prove. I laugh at myself and how I am so scientific in my approach to everything. Sometimes you have to let go and trust.

I decided on Arizona and let each school know of my decision. After I let them both know, I slept well every night.

I was working as a sales manager in the biotech industry. I was the sole breadwinner for the family and now had to make a decision to either go to medical school in the fall or most likely let go of my dream to become a doctor and the message from the spirit world. I had already deferred my entry to medical school by one year due to financial circumstances as well as still having one child living at home, and I worried I would have to retake my prerequisite classes if I didn't go, as they would soon expire. I wasn't sure what to do, as our existence and bill paying was currently weighing on my shoulders. I was in a constant quandary.

We needed to move out of our house and find renters and also find a place to live in Arizona by August. July approached, and my husband kept telling me to just go for it and things would work out. How he could be so sure, I don't know, but I'm very thankful for his optimistic view. If I had stuck with my intellectual reasoning, I'm not sure I would have enrolled. We had already exhausted our savings account and were now living paycheck to paycheck on my income. How was I supposed to just stop working? How were we to pay rent and buy food with no income coming in? I wouldn't receive any student loans until October, which would mean no income for almost two months. July came, and my husband kept telling me the job he had applied for would come through and I needed to go to medical school, as this was what I was here to do.

Always trust your gut instinct.

The Rental

We flew out to Phoenix for a weekend in July to find a house to rent, and at the same time, we put our house up for rent with a move-in date of mid-August. We put in two twelve-hour days looking all over Phoenix suburbs for a house, townhouse, or condo to rent that we would fit our family. We knew it would be tough to find a place that would allow pets. We really didn't want to have to give up the animals, as they had been with us for fifteen years.

We found a house we liked, and the real estate agent called to enquire about the property. He hung up the phone and told us they were fine with the dog but wouldn't accept the cats. We moved on and found a second house we liked. This owner was fine with the cats but wouldn't accept the dog. Our time was running out, and we really needed to find a place. We were now on our second day looking for a place, and our flight back to San Francisco was later that day. We found a third home we liked, and it was only a ten-minute commute for me to school. It was like a dream come true. This time, the real estate agent asked the real estate office what kind of pets the owner would accept, he responded with a small dog would be fine. "Great," said the real estate agent, failing to mention we had cats. We went to the office to apply. The real estate company was going to forward our application to the owner, and they would call us as soon as they found out if the owner had accepted our application.

We headed back to the airport, and as we boarded the plane and took off over Phoenix, we both stared out the window, wondering if this was all going to work out. We had made a list of other rental properties that weren't half as nice as the house we had applied for, nor the location, but at least we had a backup list. We sat silently on the plane, and I prayed it would work out.

The next day, the real estate office called us and told us the owner had accepted our application. We were so relieved. I wasn't sure how the finances were all going to work out, but all of a sudden, it all felt so real. I was going to medical school after all. I'm not really sure how we managed to get this rental, but I'm sure the Divine Universe had something to do with it. We rented a house with no income coming in after we were going to move to Phoenix, but somehow, they didn't catch it and I guess only looked at the current income.

If something is meant to happen, it will happen. Just continue to work in the direction you would like to head and try to forget all the ambiguities in your situation. Trust your soul's path.

We listed our house for rent, and it rented right away. The new tenants needed to move in by mid-August, and we needed to be out of our house by then. We contacted several moving companies that gave us a wide range of quotes differing in thousands of dollars. We finally settled on a company that had a reasonable charge.

My husband was interviewing with a company, and it looked promising that he would start working for them in September, just after we had moved to Phoenix. It was now two weeks before we were supposed to move, and I told my bosses at work that I was leaving and going to medical school. I think they were both shocked and happy for me at the same time. I ended up working full time until the day before we moved due to me being the sole income provider for the family. Every penny counted.

My last day was on a Friday, and the moving truck came Saturday morning. I was exhausted from working full time and helping with the packing every day after work for the past few weeks, but also very excited about my new path and journey. It was a mixed feeling of happiness and extreme worry and anxiety all at the same time. I again decided to have faith and trust in the Divine Universe. I felt I wouldn't have been accepted if I were not supposed to go to medical school. If I had come this far on the journey, I needed to trust it and move forward.

MESSAGE | You will never get anywhere in life if you don't take chances. The worst thing that will happen is that you fail and then you'll have to try again. Trust your soul, your messages, and your heart!

Exercise: Take time to be still and close your eyes for fifteen minutes to an hour each day, and you will start to tune in to your guides. They are always around you and willing to help you on your journey. After sitting quietly for about fifteen minutes, ask your spirit guides using your thoughts, a specific question, or sign and see what comes to your mind. Write down the question and answer you get so that later on you can verify it actually happened and it wasn't a figment of your imagination.

12

STARTING MED SCHOOL

First Day of Med School

The first day of med school finally arrived. I was both excited and nervous as I headed to the school campus. I checked in with the administrative staff and was given my ID card and other welcoming information packets. I found myself in a large lecture hall with about a hundred other medical students. I looked around nervously to see if there were any other students in my age group. I estimated the average age was around thirty-five years old. I was definitely one of the oldest students in the class and was very happy I tended to look younger than my actual age.

I kept thinking, *What have I done? My husband is still finalizing job interviews and I'm about to embark on medical school. Am I nuts? Maybe I should just leave and go find a job.* The worried thoughts kept coming. Why did I all of a sudden doubt myself? After all, I had put everything on the line for medical school, as had my husband! I wondered what the other students were thinking. Were they in as much distress as I was? I was excited to be there, but at the same time, I was torn about my decision, wondering if this was a smart idea. *Stay with it; it's too late to pull out now! I need to do this!* I thought. *After all, I feel I have been put on this path, and there must be a reason everything seems to work out even when I think it won't. If I'm meant to do this, it will work out, and I'm wasting my energy on worrying about everything, which never brings me any answers anyway. Trust in your path,* I told myself again and again. *It will all work out somehow.* As Oprah Winfrey said, "There is no greater gift you can receive or give than to honor your calling. It's why you were born and how you become most truly alive."

Orientation Week

The first week consisted of orientation and learning how to download lectures, signing in to school websites as well as icebreaker activities and other exercises. Everything was pretty easy-going, and I had no idea what I had signed up for.

During one exercise, we all sat in a circle on the floor and the microphone was passed from one person to another to share our reasons for having chosen naturopathic medical school instead of allopathic medical school. Everyone had a story. Either they had been sick and healed by naturopathic medicine or a close family member had been sick and helped by naturopathic medicine. Some were believers in a more natural holistic approach to disease. There were many touching stories, and most of us were wiping our tears as each person shared their journey. It was a beautiful moment, and I felt closer to the other students after learning about their struggles and triumphs.

Do you take time to listen to other people and their journey through life?

Med School Starts

The following week was week one of the first quarter of classes. The quarter was eleven to twelve weeks long. We were to complete around thirty-two credits of material in this short time span. That is what you do in an entire year as an undergraduate student. We were expected to complete graduate-level academics in just one-fourth of the time.

As I sat down to my first lecture, it seemed to move at hyper speed. I had thought the undergraduate prerequisite classes had moved fast, but they now seemed slow in comparison. The information flow was about fifty PowerPoint slides per hour, and we always started the day with four hours of lectures. This meant we would average two hundred PowerPoint slides per day with about one to five concepts or key terms per slide to memorize that day. It wouldn't have been too bad if that was our only class, but then we had other classes in the afternoon such as cadaver lab, physiology lab, and many days school went into the late evening hours. Some days we would get out around 9:00 p.m. only to do the same thing the next day. When was I supposed to be memorizing all the information from the four-hour-long morning lecture and afternoon classes and labs? It was extremely stressful in the beginning to get used to the speed of information. I quickly realized I needed to pay attention *all* the time, as I didn't have much time to study. The first quarter was by far the hardest in terms of getting used to the speed that I had to learn new information. I felt blasted with knowledge 24/7.

Many people ask me what it's like to start medical school at my age. I think in some ways it is easier to be the older student. I didn't require as much sleep as I had when I'd been younger. I'm not sure I would have been able to get through medical school in my twenties. I'd needed too much sleep then. I also had so much life experience to draw on, which was sometimes very helpful. However, overall, I feel that you are expected to be able to type and work on the computer and be familiar with Microsoft Office and how to download and upload documents. If you are not computer literate or can type as fast as the twenty-year-olds, I believe it would be hard. It is nothing like when I went to college during the 1980s. Because we have PowerPoint presentations and computers now, the teachers fly through the material, not to be mean, but because they have to due to the amount of information that needs to be taught.

Cadaver Lab

The day arrived when I had my first cadaver lab. Many students were slightly nervous about it, including me. After all, we were to dissect human bodies to learn anatomy. As I entered the small classroom outside the cadaver lab, I changed into my white coat.

There were model skeletons, books, and wall mounts to view x-ray film. I looked around at my classmates, and everyone looked slightly nervous. The teacher gave us clear instructions on what to expect before entering the room with the cadavers. She asked that we all divide into groups of four people. Each group was responsible for working on one cadaver. Rules about how to treat the cadavers were explained and that all tissue that may separate from the body was to be saved and kept with each individual cadaver. Nothing was to be discarded. Each cadaver was to be treated with utmost respect, and any jokes would not be tolerated, would be considered disrespectful, and could result in dismissal.

I anxiously entered the room with about eight cadavers lying on their stomachs. Together with my group members, we chose a cadaver to work on. There were typically about three teams or lab groups working on each. Other classmates who had lab at a different time were also working on the same cadavers. You were really working as a team with the other groups and where one team had left off then next team would take over to continue to dissect. As you may only have come close to the organ or nerves you were trying to identify during your lab time, you had to make sure that by the next time you entered the lab, you would need to locate what had been found by our other team members. Each group would list on a sheet what had been found during their lab time and marked the cadaver accordingly with a color-coded thread.

I looked around at my classmates in the lab, and many of the students looked pale. One person ran out of the lab, as they felt like they were going to vomit. My stomach felt queasy, and I took a deep breath to calm my nerves. After all, this was our first time in the lab, and it was an adjustment. Even though I knew they had donated their bodies to science to help us learn, it was still difficult to get used to the idea of cutting them open. It felt very invasive at first, but I knew I had to do it in order to understand and learn how the body works. I think going through cadaver lab was the best way to learn about the human body, as I gained a completely different understanding of how things look inside. Each of them had typically died from different diseases, allowing me to understand how each disease presents itself in the body. It just wouldn't have been the same seeing it on a computer. I was very grateful.

After a few weeks, the time had come when the cadavers had been flipped over to their backs and their faces were now going to be visible to me for the first time. I felt slightly anxious, as seeing their face made it more personal. Again, I learned to continue working and concentrate on the task at hand. Each time I left the lab, I thanked the cadaver for providing their body for me to learn. It may sound easy, but when you are put in a situation like this, it is most likely harder than you had imagined.

Sometimes we just have to learn to cope with our feelings in order to learn and grow. We all face challenges in our life each day regardless if we are on our path or not, but we have to learn to overcome our fears and grow from each experience.

Midterms

After about five weeks, I was already facing midterms. I looked at the schedule and realized that I had twelve midterms in five days! *How do you study for that?* I thought. Just looking at the schedule made me feel stressed. How was I supposed to pull this off and pass all those exams? I felt like I was hyperventilating just thinking about it. *Stay calm! Breathe!* I thought. I started studying and got little sleep during the following week.

Many students in the class, including myself, would share study guides. We worked together as a team, asking each other questions and sharing what we had learned. We all wanted to pass, and we had to be smart about how we studied and used our time.

I was already feeling exhausted from the first stressful five weeks of school. My first midterm was scheduled at 8:00 a.m. the next day. How was I supposed to review five weeks of material with an average of two hundred PowerPoint slides per day adding up to around a thousand PowerPoint slides per week with many items per slide to memorize? How much had I retained from class?

After taking the 8:00 a.m. exam, I would typically have one or two more exams that day. I would leave the first exam only to go directly to a study room or the library to cram for the next exam in the afternoon. Many times, I would just eat a power bar or meal shake in order to save time and get more study time. After taking the afternoon exam, I would go back to the library or study room to cram for the evening exam. After a long day of test-taking and studying, I would go home and do the exact same thing again the next day. Taking twelve exams in five days was pretty rough. Overall, I couldn't have imagined how much work was expected of me to go through a program like this, as I didn't have anything to compare it to. However, if you want something badly enough, you will find the strength to do it.

As the exam results were posted online in my personal folder, I was overjoyed to learn that I had passed all my exams! *Onward!* I thought. Some students were crying in the hallways, as they were stressed about not having done well on the exams and knew they might flunk out if they didn't do better in the finals. I wasn't the only one feeling the pressure.

Final Exams Quarter One

I had only been in school for one quarter and was already exhausted. My husband had taken a temporary job, which he was overqualified for, while waiting for final interviews for the job he wanted. We were happy to have some additional income coming in, and I trusted it would all work out. It was an extremely stressful time, both financially and academically. I again considered quitting school and going back to work to ensure we had food and shelter but remembered the message I had received and decided to stay on my current path.

Time was flying as I was kept busy 24/7, and before I knew it, finals week arrived. Again, I was faced with twelve exams in five days. As I was going through finals week, my eighty-seven-year-old mother's health was deteriorating in Sweden on the other side of the world. Her health had been declining during the last six months, and she was now almost in a coma, not very responsive, and not having any quality of life left. I prayed to my mother each night to please stay alive until I had taken the final exams. I didn't know if I could handle her passing during the week of exams and everything else that was going on in my life. I prayed she would have an easy transition and not be afraid of death, as it merely is a continuation of your soul without your body. I felt my mother could hear my prayers, and it made me feel calm and able to get a few hours of sleep.

I went from one exam to the next and then back to studying all day and night only to do the same thing the next day. I don't think I slept more than three hours per night. By the end of the week, I felt like a wrung-out sponge and was again contemplating if I was really meant to do this. As the results went up for the final exams, I was exhilarated to find out I had passed all of my classes! *Never give up*, I reminded myself. When you put everything you've got into something and then succeed, the gratitude will greater than the effort you put in.

My Mother Dies

My mother passed away just a few days after Christmas, and though I was sad to have lost her, I was relieved that she didn't have to suffer anymore. I sent her my love and thanked her for holding on through my finals.

After graduating from medical school, I became a student at Arthur Findlay College in England, which is a school of spiritualism and psychic science. My first time there in the spring of 2017, I had what is called a reading where the medium connects with a spirit in the spirit world and translates what the spirit is telling them. The medium who did my reading told me that my mother was telling her she had heard my prayers from across the world when she was passing away. That confirmation made me realize we really do continue after death and that it's merely a transition. I was elated to know that she knew all my heart was with her during her passing even though I wasn't physically able to be there. We are all connected through time and space. Never hesitate to send people your love and prayers.

Second Quarter

The second quarter of med school started January 7, 2013, after a two-week break, and I felt rested enough to tackle yet another quarter. This quarter was a continuation of the same classes we had taken in the fall. My financial situation was still stressful, and my husband had gone through several interviews with one company and had landed the job he had interviewed for which was to start in February. Things were starting to look up. When

I returned to school and entered the large lecture hall, there were so many empty seats. It looked like one-third of our class had either decided to not continue or had failed the exams and had been forced to leave school. It was an eerie feeling, and as I sat next to my friend, I felt blessed we were still in the program. Count your blessings every day to fill your heart with gratitude.

My Mother's Funeral
After two weeks into the new quarter, I left to fly to Sweden on Wednesday, January 23, with a scheduled arrival the next day in order to attend my mother's funeral on that Friday. As I arrived at my brother's house, I was happy to lie down and get some sleep before the funeral the next day.

As we arrived at the chapel where the funeral was to be held, I sat in the front row, together with my three brothers. I looked at the white coffin surrounded by flowers that contained the body of my mother. I could feel her presence and felt at ease knowing she knew I was there and how much I loved her and how proud I was of her being my mother. My oldest son had also made the trip to Sweden in order to attend the funeral, as had my nephew who was also living in the US. The service ended with everyone taking turns going up to the coffin to say our goodbyes. The most difficult moment was to see the coffin being carried out of the chapel by four strong men dressed in black. This was the final moment of my mother's existence on earth. I find it is always difficult to lose people I love, even though I know they continue to exist in the spirit world. I will still miss having them around on the earth plane.

When you lose those you love, know that their spirit is still there, and you may be able to sense their presence or even smell their perfume when they stop by for a visit. Pay attention to these moments. Even if you can't establish communication, they can hear you and you can tell them you love them and miss them. You can also ask them for a sign that they are around or okay. With your thoughts or words, ask for a sign in the next three days. It could be something like finding a feather, seeing an animal, or whatever you can think of. Then be alert and watch for this sign. If you asked for an animal, it may be a live animal, a picture, or an animal in a movie. Just look for what you asked.

Jet-lagged and exhausted, I returned to class Monday morning. I had to go back, as I had now missed three days of classes and had maxed out on the number I was allowed to miss without being held back a year. I prayed I wouldn't get sick and focused on catching up on what I had missed as well as keeping up with the pace of the week's work. After all, midterms were only two weeks away and it seemed we had just started the next quarter. There really wasn't any time for grieving, and I tried to stay focused on my studies, however difficult that was at times.

Third Quarter

This quarter was yet another quarter in the cadaver lab, more biochemistry, physiology, histology, anatomy, and more. Another twelve classes and long days at school. Not that the information we had to learn was so hard, it was just the speed of the classes that made everything so difficult, as I had to remember and retain most information after hearing it only once. This can be very challenging depending on your learning style. Whatever learning style you have, auditory, visual or kinesthetic, use your innate skill what is natural for you to help you remember. As I'm mostly a visual learner, it helped me to make a table or see a drawing, as I could easily recall the image during a test and then figure out the answer.

The midterms came after five weeks, and again, we had to take the twelve exams in five days, and there was not much time for anything else. Every week there were quizzes and smaller tests to help keep us on track so we wouldn't fall behind on studying and help us learn the material as we moved along. I'm not sure if this was helpful or not, as I still had to get a high score on each of the quizzes and sometimes it was harder to get a high score on the smaller tests as there are fewer questions. I passed the midterms, and I moved on to the second half of the second quarter.

My husband had now started his new job and had a good income. This made it easier to concentrate on school knowing everything was going to be okay money-wise. It had been a rough first couple of months, but things started to look up.

MESSAGE | Never ever give up on your dreams!

Exercise: What are your dreams? Start something that will move you toward your dream. It could be taking a class, painting, writing, playing an instrument, or anything you always wanted to do. Set time aside each day to fulfill your dreams. What makes you "tick"? Who are you? What makes you want to wake up in the morning? Write down all your dreams and then pick the one that your gut tells you to develop. You can also ask your spirit guides for help in making the next move. You have to start in order to create change and fulfill your dreams.

13

DEATH AND TRANSFORMATION

Start of Second Year

The second year of med school made me switch gears from the way I had learned to study the basic sciences to the teaching style of the new teachers and subjects. I was anxious about the rumors I had heard about how tough some of the exams and teachers were. I couldn't flunk out of medical school now, as I was already a year into the program. The teachers were, of course, very good, despite their reputations.

After I found out I had passed one of these tough classes, I said to my daughter, "Knowing I got a passing grade, I could have porcupines for dinner!" She, of course, laughed hysterically at my statement, as she understood what I meant. It had been a tough class to pass.

The scenario for this year was the same as year one: several hours of lectures in the morning, with the same number of PowerPoint slides followed by another ten to eleven classes. The workload was once again overbearing. The number of credits we carried was around twenty-eight credits in eleven weeks. I was excited to begin my second year and felt like I had everything under control, not knowing or understanding how much work lay ahead.

Clinic Entry Exam

The first two quarters went by quickly, as I really didn't have much time for anything but studying. I was being pushed even harder now, as I had to prepare to enter clinic rotations the following fall. My physical exam skills and ability to recognize symptoms and diseases were being honed.

That spring, I had to take what was called the clinic entry exam. During a clinic entry exam, the school had arranged pretend patients to play the role of my patient, complaining of some symptom that I was then supposed to recognize and pretend to treat. I was told what time I was to be in the clinic and upon arrival was directed to one of the classrooms in the clinic together with other students. My hands were cold and clammy, as I was nervous about the exam. I had been preparing for this test for the past few weeks, and a lot was at stake. There was no talking allowed between the students, and there was a doctor monitoring the classroom. When it was my turn to see my pretend patient, a resident physician came to escort me to the exam room. I was given a time limit of an average patient visit for my test.

I was only allowed a blank piece of paper or a blank document on my computer to write down my chart notes, and I had to show the doctor I had closed all other screens and Internet connection on my computer. I had memorized the correct order to ask my patients questions and was ready to begin as the doctor started the timer.

I started firing questions to my patient while I was typing furiously, trying to make sure I was asking all the pertinent questions that could be related to the symptoms this pretend patient stated he was experiencing. The patient will not give you any extra information; they will only answer the questions you ask. In the real world, I think it is easier to draw conclusions, as the patient typically talks to you more. After I finished asking questions, the doctor asked which possible diagnoses I had in mind, why I had come to this conclusion, and which physical exam I would like to perform based on what I had learned so far about the patient. He also asked what imaging and labs I would like to order. After relaying this information to the doctor, I was told to proceed and perform the physical exam I had chosen. This was, of course, a very stressful event, as I had to try to put everything together that I had been taught so far.

This was my introduction to clinic rotations, and they evaluated me to make sure I was ready for what lay ahead. After I passed the clinic entry exam, I was ready to start assisting the upperclassmen on shift and I was officially given my white coat during what was called the white coat ceremony. This was a big event and milestone, as I had now passed the core sciences of medical school and was ready to start learning on clinic shift rotations seeing real patients.

The White Coat Ceremony

The white coat ceremony was held off-campus, and all my kids were present. Each student was called up on stage and presented with their white coat. As they called my name and I stepped up on stage, I was so proud! Suddenly medical school seemed more real than ever. There I was, with a white coat and stethoscope around my neck! I could hear my kids yelling and cheering as I walked down the aisle to the back of the room. *WOW! Never ever give up on your dreams! Hard work and persistence do pay off!* I thought.

Spring Quarter

After completing the second year of medical school, you take what are called the board exams. There are two board exams you have to pass in medical school. The first exam is taken after the first two years and covers the basic sciences. The second board exam is taken after you complete medical school and covers the clinical concepts. As I completed my second year of medical school, I had a two-week break in July before starting the next quarter. How could I study two years' worth of material in two weeks? As I knew I needed more than two weeks to review all that material, I started studying for the board exams during the spring quarter. I was also faced with extra classes pertaining to the clinic entry exam during the spring, so a lot of extra work and stress were added to my life. I think this was one of the most stressful quarters during my journey through medical school.

There were several books I used to review what I had learned during the first two years. One book was called the *USMLE*, or the *United States Medical Licensing Exam, Part One*. I made sure I knew everything listed in this book as well as the medical licensing exam books specifically for naturopathic physicians, as we learn other things not covered in allopathic medical school. I would make up a schedule for how many pages to review each day for the next three months to make sure I would have seen all the material once before taking the exam in August.

It was during this spring quarter with the extra study load and pressure of classes and exams that my marriage started to fall apart.

When I entered medical school, they told us that there is a high rate of separation during the very challenging academic program, but I didn't think it would happen to me. The tension grew between my husband and me, and I had very little time to spend with him, as my schedule was overflowing with work. We had already started to grow apart before entering medical school, and this extra pressure and stress made it too hard to try and hold an already fragile relationship together. I kept telling my husband that I couldn't discuss our relationship until after the board exam at the beginning of August as I already knew what would result from this discussion and felt it was too much to deal with at the time. He was very understanding, and we got along fine. We both felt we had grown apart over the last few years, so there really wasn't a rush to try to resolve any conflicts between us four weeks before my board exams. We both knew we had to hold off on any deeper discussion.

Basic Science Board Exam

The next quarter of classes started, and during the first or second week of classes, we had one day that had been slotted for taking the board exam. The board exams are given at the same time across the United States. I had prepared for this exam for the previous few months and was hoping I knew enough to pass. The exam was being held at an offsite location, and I had packed power bars and a drink, as I was allowed to bring them with me into the exam hall. I was nervous about the exam and prayed I had studied enough to pass.

Upon arriving at the testing site, I had to show my driver's license and registration papers. Once I was signed in, I had to proceed to wardrobe and give them my backpack and cell phone. I wasn't even allowed to bring my own pencil. Once they opened the doors, I again showed my driver's license to be identified and was then escorted to my seat in the big hall. There was plenty of room between the seats to avoid any kind of cheating.

Once all the students were seated, they handed out the tests and put them upside down on our desk. We were not to touch the paper until instructed to do so. Once everyone had a test in front of them, they asked us to turn it over and start entering our names and social security number on the front page of the test but not to start the exam. Once everyone had completed filling out their names, they allowed us to start the exam and started the timer. I said a silent prayer: *Please let me pass this test!* All I could do was try my best. Had I retained enough information from the last two most hectic years of my life to be able to recall the correct answer on the test? After all, most of it was memory recall, as it was the basic science boards. How many times had I thought I wasn't going to pass a test in the past two years but then still pulled it off? I needed to do the same with this test, as intimidating as it seemed to be sitting in this big hall with a test so thick it resembled a small book.

I looked around at my friends scattered throughout the big auditorium. Everyone was hunched over the desk and ready to start. *Trust your instincts,* I thought as I proceeded to the first page of the exam. I knew I most likely wouldn't have much time to go back to reread questions, as there were way too many. I figured I only had about one minute per question. It only took me around fifteen to thirty seconds to read each question, so if I knew the answer immediately, I would save time on these questions. However, if I needed to think about the answer to many questions, I would be pressed for time. I decided to go with my gut instinct and answer the question even if I wasn't sure of the answer and put a little mark next to the question on the answer sheet, should I have time to go back and review those questions. I just hoped all the questions would not end up having a mark next to them! I took a deep breath and began. Sometimes when I read the answers to a question, I would be able to narrow it down to two possible answers. Each time this happened, I felt adrenalin rush through my veins. I would put a little mark in the margin of the question and move on. *Just do your best! Focus on one question at a time and breathe,* I told myself. If I failed, I would have to take the test again. Three hours later, I was done with the first part of the exam and had a one-hour break to eat lunch. I had brought some food along in a cooler and ate it outside with some friends.

I wouldn't find out if I had passed the boards until eight weeks later, as there was a big procedure around the correction of this national test. As I handed in my exam at the end of the day, I was so relieved the first boards were over and again prayed I had passed. If I didn't pass the exam, I would have to keep taking it every six months until I passed, and as it costs several hundred dollars to take it, there is both an economic burden as well as a time constraint. I really wanted to pass it the first time I took it.

The Spiritual Fair

The weekend that followed the board exam, my daughter and I went to a local spiritual fair. It was a fun and welcomed event after the grueling months of hard work and preparation for the boards and clinic entry.

I decided to try different things and started with a card reading. The lady told me I had problems with my marriage. *Wow, maybe she tells everyone this and sometimes gets it right?* I thought to myself. I moved on to several other stations at the exhibit for different types of spiritual readings, but the same message came across each time. *Wow, how strange; is this a fluke?* I thought. Why were they all telling me the same thing? I thought that maybe it was just a common problem and they told everyone this and hoped they would get it right. Could it be that they were actually picking up on something? My left brain was in overdrive trying to figure out how they could know this information about me. My brain kept asking questions. Were they actually reading me? Was this something I could do as well? Could anybody learn this?

The Discussion

Later that week, my husband and I sat down to discuss our

problems. Even though we had enjoyed our marriage, we both felt unhappy with our current situation. We needed to move on, following our own path. We needed to part ways in order to allow ourselves the freedom in life we both so desperately yearned for. As it was August and I was in the middle of a quarter and the kids had already decided to be with us during the Christmas holidays, we decided it would be better if we gave ourselves some time to think this decision through and be together one final time for the holiday season. We slept in separate rooms to see how we felt; after all, we had been married for thirty-six years and we were questioning if our decision to separate was right. Was it just the stress of medical school that had brought this on, or would we have decided to separate anyway? I was sad about our decision, but at the same time, it felt good and right.

Board Exam Results

We finally approached the week when the results for the board exams were being mailed. Each day, I anxiously waited for the mailman. Some of my friends had already received their results, and I kept praying I had passed. Finally, one day when I went to the mailbox, I found an envelope with my results inside. I was afraid of opening it on the street, as I felt like I would faint if I hadn't passed. I carried the letter back to the house and sat at the kitchen table. I carefully opened the envelope, my hands shaking, and found out I had passed my basic science boards! I was so relieved I had tears of happiness rolling down my face. It was a huge confidence boost to know I had passed the first boards and was moving on. *I can do this!* I thought. Small steps lead to bigger steps.

The rest of the fall flew by, and before I knew it, the Christmas holiday break arrived. The boys joined us from California, and we spent our last holiday together as a family. It was bittersweet. We had decided that the best time for my husband to move out would be between Christmas and New Year's, as this was when we both had time off. After the boys left, he started packing up all the things we had decided he would take. He had already found a place to live and was returning to California. I felt sad our relationship was coming to an end. It seemed surreal watching him pack his car. Had we made the right decision?

Separations

We still had our little Lhasapoo, Elvis, whose health had been deteriorating for the previous few years. He had both of his eyes removed due to glaucoma and was having problems with his heart. He would wake us at night when he was finding it difficult to breathe, and we had taken him to the vet several times. We knew we were now keeping him alive for ourselves and we needed to think about what was best for him. He was now sixteen and a half years old, and we decided we needed to put him down to relieve his suffering. This was very difficult, as this was our last dog that was still alive and whom we loved so much. Not only did we both grieve the fact that we had to put him down, but this also served as a significant symbol to the end of our relationship and all the fun years we'd had with the kids, dogs, and cats. It reminded me of all the times we had played the guitar together in the kitchen only to watch our dogs fall asleep to the music. So many good memories were coming to an end. I again questioned if I had made the right decision. We were both crying looking at each other as our tears were streaming down our faces as we returned to our car. It was a very difficult moment.

When we got back to the house, we continued to divide things up and pack so my husband could leave the next day.

We were both silent and grieving. I had a feeling of emptiness in my stomach, like a black hole, as if part of me were gone. My husband would jokingly say that maybe this was wrong and he would be coming back crawling on his knees begging me to take him back in a few years. I wasn't sure myself. Was I being unreasonable because of all the stress I was experiencing in school? After all, they had warned us at the start of the program that it is a terrible strain on relationships.

After my husband left the next day, I was both sad and elated. I was sad to be parting ways but elated the stress we had experienced was coming to an end. Just like when people are sick and don't have a diagnosis, it wears on them. It often feels better to have a diagnosis so you now know what you are trying to cure. It was a similar feeling. I had now officially separated. It was done. I had to move on.

The Bed
As there were a few other separations in my class, I had learned from another woman to get a new bed after going through a separation, as there are too many memories in the bed I had slept in with my husband. That evening, the same day my husband left, my daughter and I went to a store to purchase a queen-size wooden bed. We carried all the pieces of the bed upstairs to my bedroom. The worst part was the queen-size mattress. As neither of us are the muscular type, it was too heavy for us to lift. We dragged and pushed this mattress and laughed so hard we had tears rolling down our faces, as we were constantly dropping it as we tried to maneuver it up the curved staircase. After a long night of putting the bed frame together, it was now almost 2:00 a.m. and we were so tired and giggly, everything seemed funny. We made several attempts to lift the queen mattress on to the bed, the final step of assembly, but we dropped it several times,

and each time we failed at putting the mattress on the bed we would laugh more and more to the point where our muscles just didn't want to work at all! The laughter was a good relief for all the tension we had both experienced for the past few weeks and especially during the past few days. After all, it's important to see the humor in the small things in life.

Don't let the big problems get you down. See the humor in everyday life. Life really isn't that serious. We make it serious.

The Astrologer

The following week, I had my first reading with an astrologer. She arrived at my house, and as she was squirming in her seat while reading my astrological chart, she said there was some turmoil in my relationship. After I told her I had just separated from my husband, she took a deep breath and a smile appeared on her face. She asked when the marital problems began, and I told her last year in April when I was under a lot of stress for the clinic entry exam as well as board preparation. I then told her how we had decided to separate in August and how my husband had moved out during the last week in December. Her response was that it was all in my chart. She showed me it had started in April followed by more problems in August and that it culminated in December. As this was my first experience with astrology, it really threw me for a loop. Had this been decided before I was born? Was this part of my destiny and earthly experience? Was this what I had signed up for in this life? How could she see this in my chart? It made me think of life differently. How much of our life can be seen in an astrology chart? I was amazed.

Polarity Class

About a week after my astrology reading, I signed up for a week-end class in polarity at the school my daughter was attending, as I was eager to learn more about the energy and polarity of our bodies. There were probably around forty to fifty students in this class, and during the last day of the class, the teacher asked how many of those attending the class had experienced an NDE in the past. To everyone's surprise, about twenty people raised their hands. How was this possible? I had only met one person in twenty-five years who'd had an NDE, and here we were all gathered in the same class in a suburb of Phoenix. I was in awe, and as the teacher led us in a meditation ending with ohm, it was absolutely magical. A sound I've never heard in any other gathering of a meditation. Why was it so different? Was it because so many of us had experienced an NDE? It was the sound I'd always craved to hear since my NDE. The sound of the Universe.

Third Quarter, Year Three

I was now halfway through my third year in medical school, and it was January 2015. This year is what I refer to as the year of death, as everything I had always loved died or fell away from me. Even though my physical separation from my husband took place two days before New Year, as well as putting our dog to sleep, I count it as part of 2015.

As we had now officially separated, the rent was too expensive in the big house I was living in, and we needed to downsize to be able to afford the two rentals, one for my husband and one for my daughter and me. My daughter and I had to go through all the things that were still left, and I sold anything that wouldn't fit in the condo on Craigslist. It was a hectic time, as I had to constantly list things and then sell them while keeping my husband in the loop. We still shared all expenses, as we were still married, and I divided up any money equally for any sale made. Some of my friends told me I should keep the money, as I was doing all the work, but that didn't feel right to me, and I wanted a clear conscience. After all, he was still helping to support me, and we had a good relationship. Why would I be dishonest? Honesty always wins in the end. If you know in your heart that you have done what is right, then that will bring you peace regardless of what other people may think of your actions.

After two months of sorting out our furniture as well as looking for a place to live, my daughter and I found a great two-bedroom condo only ten minutes from where we were living and still the same distance to school for both of us. We arranged for the move to take place during the first week of the next quarter before the school load would get too heavy. We weren't able to move during the one-week school break, as we didn't have access to the condo until the following week. I was anxious to get settled in to the new place so I could move forward with my new life. I finally felt I had been given a fresh start. After another two weeks of going between the old house to get carpets cleaned, paint touch-ups, and cleaning up, we were finally out of the house and I could focus on school again.

You can create new beginnings by moving or simply rearranging the furniture and pictures in your home. Creating a new space can help in transitioning from your old self to your new self.

The Fire

I was exhausted from all the work of moving and separating and thought the worst was over, but I had no idea that it was just the beginning of a horrendous year.

One night, during the first week of living in the condo, my daughter stormed into my bedroom at 3:00 a.m. yelling, "Mom, there is a fire. Talk to the nine-one-one lady!" She handed me the cell phone and said, "We have to make sure the grandma gets out," and she took off running with her boyfriend across the greenbelt wearing shorts and a tank top. I grabbed the cell phone, and the 911 operator asked with whom she was speaking and what the emergency was. I squeezed the cell phone between my ear and shoulder while hopping down the hallway on one foot as I desperately pulled on my sweatpants. As I ran barefoot through the greenbelt at full speed, following my daughter and her boyfriend, pressing the cell phone against my ear, I told 911 that there was a fire in a condo and that I could smell smoke. As I continued to run, I saw a police officer running from the street into our greenbelt toward the condo. I reported the activity to 911 and kept running. As I arrived in front of the condo, I could see the flames through the living room window. The lady at the dispatch center asked for my address to confirm the location of the fire. Within seconds, we could hear the sirens. We watched the firefighters working as fast as they could while trying to contain the blaze. As the windows blew out on the condo, the TV news station arrived to interview those involved. The TV station asked to interview me, but I declined, as I didn't want to be seen on the morning news wearing a worn-out tank top and sweatpants with my hair looking like Einstein's! By the time the fire had been put out and the TV crews, which were stationed right outside my condo, finally left, it was morning and time to attend yet another day of classes.

It seemed that every week something happened. When was it all going to end? Sometimes life is so full of events that we can barely keep up with our daily chores. Always remember that these situations are transient.

My Brother-in-Law

About two weeks went by, and at the end of April, my brother-in-law passed away. We were told he was in his final stages of life and would most likely pass in the following two weeks. This was the husband of my sister-in-law, whom my father had asked to look after me when I moved to the United States in my early twenties. He had always had an important place in my heart. The evening before he passed, I knew his death was near and felt as though he was in and out of his body and visiting me in my room. I was so sad that it was his time to leave and exhausted from all that had happened during the past few months. I fell asleep with tears rolling down my cheeks.

We are all connected through time and space, and you have probably had similar experiences in your life.

The next day, he passed away. I was very saddened by this loss, but it was his time to move on to the other side. The weeks that followed were, of course, filled with grief as I continued to try to keep up with the demanding studies of school.

US Citizen

Two days after my brother-in-law passed, May 1, 2015, my boys and husband arrived in Phoenix to attend my ceremony at the courthouse where I would officially become a US citizen. I had put my application in for citizenship the previous fall when we decided we were separating, as I had only had a green card for all the years I had been married. Needless to say, it was a big day for the family and myself.

I also took back my maiden name, as I wanted to honor my family and become Dr. Valentin just like my father, brother, and cousin. I think the name change also helped me find myself in my heart, as going through a separation after so many years of marriage made me question who I was. As I took my oath in the courthouse with all the other applicants, I felt so proud to become a citizen. To me, the United States had always represented the land of the free with liberty and justice for all.

Memorial Service

About a week later, I flew to Texas to attend my brother-in-law's memorial service. It was the weekend right after the midterms, and as I had been taking tests all week, there was no big study load that weekend and everything worked out perfectly. It was a beautiful service, and it felt good to see my extended family on my husband's side for the first time since the separation. Just because we weren't living together anymore didn't mean the relationship I had with my extended family would change. Always keep those you love in your relationships.

Pounce the Cat

It had been a busy couple of months, and I was just barely hanging on and keeping up with the workload. As I entered June, there were only a few weeks left of the quarter, and I was looking forward to a break. I approached finals week, and one of our cats that originally belonged to my middle child stopped eating, and his behavior became strange. He was now seventeen years old. I knew something was terribly wrong and that his time on earth had come to an end. I called the vet from my car while driving home from school and explained the situation. I was so exhausted from the previous few months that I had nothing left. I could barely keep it together on the phone. I was so sad about the possibility of losing something else. As soon as I arrived home and looked at the cat, I started crying.

My daughter said, "Don't worry, Mom, I can take him to the vet." I firmly stated that I would be fine as soon as I had something to eat. But as soon as I thought of putting him down, I would start crying. I was really at the end of my rope. I didn't want anything else I had loved to leave me.

My daughter brought Pounce to the vet, and it turned out he had a very fast-growing tumor in his throat which was preventing him from eating and accounting for his strange behavior. She put him down, and he joined his other pet family members in pet heaven. I was so thankful for her brave assistance and realized she was now a grown-up and fully capable of handling things on her own. Sometimes it takes a crisis in order to realize there is help available.

The Uncle

July finally came, and this was the quarter I only had clinic rotations. It was a welcomed change after the past year of struggles. I had arranged for some clinic rotations in private clinics in the area as well as at school to get a better idea of how private clinics operate.

During this month, yet another close relative passed away; it was my husband's uncle. I had always thought of him as my own uncle, as I had known him since I was seventeen years old. He had been part of our wedding ceremony in Sweden in 1979. He was a Lutheran minister, and we had an American minister and a Swedish minister at our wedding ceremony. Even though he was in his eighties, his death was unexpected and sudden. I felt numb. Why was everyone dying or leaving? I was thankful for the astrologer who had told me during my reading back in January that the year ahead was going to be a rocky year and things were going to fall away from me, but also open new paths in my life. I reminded myself of this yet again, as I'd been in constant grieving mode since January.

IANDS

The whole month of August went by with no memorial service and nothing dying. I was so grateful! It was during this month that I attended my first IANDS (International Association of Near-Death Studies) conference. One of the speakers was

Suzanne Giesemann, former Navy commander of the United States, who had become a well-known evidential medium and author of several books on the topic. I was intrigued by her abilities to communicate with the spirit world. I wondered how she did that on demand. I decided to attend her lecture over others that were offered at the same time. I had never seen a medium at work and was very critical in my beliefs regarding how she would prove she had contact with someone in the spirit world versus just saying something that could apply to most people.

The first picture she put up was a picture of Arthur Findlay College in England where she had studied and developed her mediumship skills. I looked at that image and immediately knew I must go there. My brain quickly took over and said, *You are crazy! You can't go there. You haven't even graduated from medical school yet, and then you have to pass the boards, find a job, and build your practice.*

She started her lecture, and I was very intrigued by her abilities to prove whom she was communicating with within the spirit world by giving detailed information about the spirit she was communicating with that she couldn't have known unless she had known the spirit during life. It was thirteen months later that I met the new friend who told me she was communicating with my mother and that I was to go take a class at Arthur Findlay College.

Sometimes we get messages, but our brain gets in the way of allowing ourselves to listen and trust. Pay attention to your messages.

September
September came, and a close family friend in Sweden passed away. This was someone who had always been very important

to me during my life, my father's best friend. We had spent many holidays and vacations together, and as a child, I would always think that if I lost my father, I wished he would be my father. He was very close to my heart. As the funeral took place in Sweden and was being held at a time I wouldn't be able to leave medical school, I had to let go of the thought of attending in person. During the past two years, I have received messages from him through other mediums, and I know he is still around me and watches over me.

You are never alone. The people you were close to and loved when they were alive are most likely around you trying their best to give you support and love.

Death and Transformation

It had been a year full of grief, but with any kind of death, there is transformation. It could be a physical death of a person, death of a job, death of an animal, death of a relationship, or anything else that comes to an end. It is in the darkness that new creation and new beginnings take form. We are created in the dark womb. A seed grows in the darkness of the earth. We renew as we close our eyes and go to sleep each night. It is from the darkness that we create, renew, and transform. Things will always fall away from us in life, and even though these moments create a lot of sorrow, they also provide an opportunity for growth, reflection, and transformation that would otherwise not have taken place. Remember to always keep a positive outlook in life, especially when you go through difficult times.

"Positive Thinking"

Don't ever give up.
Always think positively.
Imagine yourself doing things you think you can't do.
Never assume anything negative.
Always assume the positive.

There is always room for improvements.
Don't take anything for granted.
Life is precious.
Imagine yourself doing well.

Always look ahead.
Never look back.
Live in the moment.
Enjoy what each day brings.
Keep your chin up, even when you feel you've come to an end.

Don't listen to other people.
Do what you feel is right.
Stand up for your own rights.
Only you are in charge of your life.
Make your life what you want it to be.

ACV

MESSAGE | The darkness holds the power of creativity and transformation. It is from the darkness that new life awakens and begins.

Exercise: When you feel like you can barely take another day of life and nothing seems to be going in the right direction, remind yourself that this, too, shall pass. Tell yourself that you are strong. Remind yourself that you are sowing your seeds and soon your flowers will blossom. Send yourself an email with this message or write it down and put it on your mirror or wall to remind yourself daily.

14

FINAL YEAR OF MED SCHOOL

First Quarter of Last Year in Med School

The first quarter of the last year in med school started, and I was so excited to be nearing the end of this journey. On a Friday evening in October after school, I flew to Boston and met up with my ex-husband to attend the memorial service for my husband's beloved uncle who had passed away in July. It was a beautiful service and wonderful to meet all the relatives on my husband's side of the family whom I had known since I was a teenager. The weekend flew by, and before I knew it, I was back in class.

Two weeks after the memorial service, my mother-in-law, the uncle's older sister, passed away. It was as if they had arrived at the earth plane together and left together. I was again at the end of my rope and not sure how much more grief I could bear. It felt like someone had squeezed my heart for so long it had shattered into pieces. My mother-in-law was in her nineties, and I knew it was her time to move on to the other side, as her health had been deteriorating over the previous few years. Nevertheless, it was as difficult losing my mother-in-law as losing my own mother during the first year of medical school. My mother-in-law had been my spiritual guide on earth, and I had always felt very close to her. In many ways, I was much more like my mother-in-law than my own mother.

I lay down on the bed and wondered if I had made the right decision to separate from my husband. Everyone I had loved so much was gone and no longer part of my life. I would think of how my mother-in-law and father-in-law had separated for about two years when my husband was around twelve years old, but then they decided to get back together. Was that something I was now experiencing? Was I not seeing all the good things we had together? After all, we had been married for thirty-six years. I remembered the speech I'd given to my mother-in-law and father-in-law on their sixtieth wedding anniversary in 2003. I got out of bed and looked in the special folder in the filing cabinet that contained family memorabilia to see if I still had a copy of it. To my surprise, I found it. It was still in the folder where I had put it many years ago. As I read it, I remembered all the fun times and how life has its ups and downs just like it had for my parents-in-law. I laughed out loud as I read my speech and thought of how much I missed them.

Sixtieth-Anniversary Speech

Etta, my mother-in-law.
John, my father-in-law.
My "adopted" American parents.
The ones I've known for twenty-eight years.
It's their special mark today.
A special mark in their life.
A mark of accomplishment.
A mark of strength.
A mark that shows that things are possible.
A mark of an instinct deep inside them.
It's their mark, the mark of staying married for sixty years!

I remember when I first came to their family.
Three large muddy dogs in the kitchen.
John at the kitchen table, trying to get his breakfast down in
thirty seconds or less.
John, worried he would miss his train.
Etta, stepping over the dogs while frying eggs and "yelling"
for the kids to get ready.
Both of them, sharing the kitchen space together.

The first time I visited them, I was eighteen years old.
Being a blond tan Swedish girl dressed in short shorts, I got
the looks from the man in the house.
I could read his face; it said something like, "Gee, my son
must be thinking about that number after five,"
which in Swedish is the number "sex,"
"I'll bet she doesn't know anything practical, like how to
use a tool."

He told me to follow him to the basement.

I remember thinking, *Wow! This is amusing.*

He probably thinks I don't know how to use a tool!

We went down the steep stairway to the basement

where John proceeded to hold up a screwdriver in front of me

and asked,

"Do you know what this is?"

I smiled and thought,

I wonder what "skruvmejsel" is called in English!

It's not one of those useful words they taught me in English class!

I told him I didn't know the name for it.

He smiled and said clearly, "Oh, it's called a

SCREWDRIVER."

He then asked if I knew how to use it.

I told him I did!

He looked at me in disbelief and got some screws out and

asked me to show him.

I neatly screwed the screws into place.

He looked rather surprised, as if he really hadn't expected me

to know how to USE the screwdriver!

I looked at him and smiled.

His face was saying, "Wow, maybe she isn't as dumb as I first

thought,

but I bet she won't know how to use a saw!"

He took out the saw and asked the same question he had

asked about the screwdriver,

He held up the saw and asked, "Do you know what this is?"

I smiled and thought, *I wonder what "sag" is called in English.*

It's not one of those useful words they taught me in English class!

Again, I had to use the saw to prove I knew what I was doing.

We proceeded with this test for about half an hour,

after which time John was pleased to find out I did know

something about tools!
We went back upstairs to the kitchen to announce that I had
passed the "tool test."
I think it was after this test that I was officially inaugurated
to the family!

Etta, on the other hand, didn't ask me to pass a tool test,
No, with Etta, it was all about passing a mental test!
I had to learn to NOT ask before getting an animal.
"Don't ask; just get it," she would say!
Which explains why we now have a small farm at our house!
Etta has taught me many things.
She taught me how to cook a turkey,
she taught me what books to use when teaching my children,
and she taught me how to rebel!
Not many mothers-in-law will teach you that last lesson, how
to be a protestor!
No, that one belongs to MY mother-in-law, and I'm proud of it!
I had to learn about all sorts of diets and self-improvement
techniques;
I had to learn to keep up with her constantly changing
thought pattern,
new lifestyles, and her new philosophies about life itself!
It has been a lot of fun riding on her train, and I enjoy my
wild-spunky-hippy-like-mother-in-law very much;
the world wouldn't be the same without her, and I always
wonder before
she comes for a visit what she has gotten herself into this time!
I think I'll keep her!
There aren't many like her around!

Their life, it's like a train,
climbing steep mountains during a storm,
gliding through the valleys on a perfect summer day,
passenger, getting on and off,
entering and leaving their lives.
As they've been riding their train,
they've been exchanging ideas with their friends, family,
and each other,
and they've grown through their experiences both together
and apart,
leading their friends and offspring by example,
leading us, showing us that things are possible even when
times get tough.
They have both done what they knew they had to do;
they stayed together through their life because they know,
they know that the two of them together are stronger than one.

Happy sixtieth anniversary to Etta and John, a couple that is
leading us all by example!
I love you both very much!

I'm sharing this story so you will take the time to show appreciation for the people you love! Before you know it, they may all be gone. When was the last time you told the people you care about that you care about them and how much they mean to you? Take that time. Give someone a hug. Tell them you love them!

I went back to bed and wondered if I had I made a mistake letting my husband off the hook so easily. Should I have been more resistant and tried to work things out? Why was everyone dying and leaving me? I only had six months left of medical school, and nothing was the same as when I'd started only four years ago. What was the purpose of it all in the long run? Was it supposed to be this way? After all, I reminded myself again that the astrologer had told me things would fall away and new paths and doors would open in my life, and it helped me cope.

I believe that sometimes we have to go through difficult times, which may cause emotionally painful experiences, in order to create our new paths. I felt like I was cutting down branches in a deep forest, sweating, crying, and using all the strength I could muster up to continue paving my path. But I knew as I was creating this new path through the deep woods, there would be sunshine and a nice meadow waiting on the other side of the forest. Sometimes, when we feel like everything is falling apart and we are about ready to give up, our most important lessons and stamina will emerge from the experience, making us stronger and more confident human beings in the end.

I took a deep breath and reminded myself that tough situations never last forever. Then I wiped away my tears and closed my eyes.

Slinky

A week before the memorial service for my mother-in-law in Fort Lauderdale, Florida, Slinky's health deteriorated. She had been my oldest son's cat and was now eighteen years old. My daughter and I took her to the vet to have her put down. It was the last of the pets to pass to the other side, and my mother-in-law's memorial service was the last memorial service while going through medical school.

Life had been a whirlwind. However, nothing lasts forever. It all seemed unfair and depressing at the time, but looking back, I now understand how strong these experiences have made me. Sometimes our experiences don't make sense when we are going through hard times; only later as we reflect on what we learned do we understand the lessons of life.

It was a welcomed change to have more clinic rotations than classes in the classroom these final quarters. It was always so rewarding to see patients improve and get better and made the whole stressful experience of attending medical school worth it. I was so excited that in a few months I would have earned the title of doctor and would now be able to help people feel better all day long. This is what I was meant to do in life. It's never too late to follow your dreams.

Graduation

The last quarter of med school flew by, and before I knew it, I was walking out of my final exam. It was an incredible feeling of relief. I had made it. It was surreal. All that was left was the clinical boards.

The graduation ceremony was on June 25, 2016, exactly thirty years after the birth of my first child. On the day he was born, I could not in my wildest imagination have thought that I would graduate from medical school on that exact day thirty years later.

All my kids attended my graduation ceremony, as did my husband and my two sisters-in-law. I arrived at the auditorium early in the morning, where the graduation was to take place. It all seemed surreal. I put on my gown and hat and walked into the auditorium to my seat. We had been assigned seats in alphabetical order. The graduation ceremony started, and the students lined up on the side of the stage and waited for their name to be called. As my last name began with a V, I was going to be one of the last to be called. After watching my friends, it was finally my turn to line up. As they called, "Doctor Valentin," I felt so proud! Not only had I achieved my dream, but I was also honored to be representing my father, who had been my role model growing up. I had grown up being used to waking in the middle of the night as the phone would ring when my father was on call. I would hear my father answering, "Doctor Valentin," and he always sounded like he had been awake, even though it was 3:00 a.m. It seemed unreal I was now being called by the same name and title. I walked up the steps onto the stage to receive my doctorate degree. Here I was, fifty-eight years old, earning the title of NMD. *Nothing is impossible! Follow your dreams! It's never too late!* I thought as I shook the president's hand.

Clinical Boards

After taking a few days off to celebrate, I was back to the grind. I had to pass the clinical medical boards that were scheduled for the first week of August. I had one month to study.

The clinical exam boards were to take place over three days, compared to the science boards, which I had completed in one day of testing. I had already been studying and reviewing material since the springtime, but now I needed to really focus. I again studied out of the *USMLE, United States Medical Licensing Exam, Part Two*, as well as *National Study Guides for Naturopathic Physicians*. The core clinical exams were scheduled from eight to twelve each of the three days. I also had to prepare for the acupuncture boards as well as minor surgery boards, which were scheduled as the afternoon exams for day one and two. There was a lot of material to review, and just looking at the pile of books and study sheets made me feel stressed. How was I supposed to know everything and review everything in such a short amount of time? I told myself that being stressed about it wasn't going to help, and remaining calm and focused was a better option. All I could do was try my best. If I had made it this far, I could pass the final clinical boards, too. It seemed never-ending, but the finish line was close, and I mustered up my final ounce of strength to keep going.

The core clinical exam consisted of about 130 to 135 questions each day. It was exhausting, as each of the questions typically consisted of a full eight-and-a-half-by-eleven sheet of the scenario of a clinical presentation of a patient case followed by another page of about four to five multiple-choice questions pertaining to the case presented. After I read all the cases and questions, my mind felt like it was going into melt down. The one-hour lunch break before attacking the afternoon exam was welcomed. In the afternoon of the first two days of testing, I took the acupuncture boards one day and the minor surgery boards the next day. The third day of testing consisted of only the core clinical exams from eight to twelve, and I was finally done with the exam process.

After four years of studying and taking board exams, I was ready for a break, but I needed to earn money so started working right away the following Monday. I was excited to have a job but now had to wait until the beginning of October to find out if I had even passed all the sections on my medical boards. It was a nerve-wracking wait, and time seemed to pass slowly.

Finally, the mail came with my results. Again, I was afraid of opening the letter and took it inside and sat in the rocking chair. What would happen if I hadn't passed? I shuddered at the thought. I took a deep breath and opened the envelope. I carefully reviewed each of the five sections I needed to have passed as well as the acupuncture and minor surgery sections and let out a scream of excitement as I realized I had passed! I immediately texted my family and close friends to let them know. I was so excited! I was issued my medical license on October 13, 2016, and as I stared at my license, I thought, *Listen to your heart! Follow that dream! Nothing is impossible!*

**MESSAGE | It's never too late to make a change and
follow your heart.**

Exercise: Small steps lead to bigger steps. Take initiative and
start the process of working toward your goal. It doesn't matter
how old you are. If we live to be one hundred years old and you
are fifty right now, you haven't even lived half of your adult life
yet. Be brave and take a step toward change, as once you start
rolling your snowball, it will gain momentum, and after a while,
it will roll by itself.

15

THE JOURNEY OF SELF-LOVE

Affirmations

Going through medical school was not only a journey to become a doctor but also a journey of my soul. Much self-reflection took place during those years.

If you are a woman, you may feel the need to be beautiful, thin, and attractive in order to be loved. If you are not of good proportions as established by society and magazines, you may feel like you don't fit in or that you are not attractive. Being attractive as established by our society usually indicates having a big chest, straight teeth, nice hair, and a thin figure. However, true beauty is not what your eyes see. Beauty comes from within. Then why is it so hard for many to trust their inner beauty? Your outer physical appearance and beauty come from the beauty you hold within your heart and soul. Be happy with the body you were given in this lifetime. If you feel a need to change or alter it, ask yourself if you truly love yourself. Do you think you are beautiful? How can you truly love other people if you are not accepting and loving yourself? Every night before you go to sleep and every morning when you wake up, put your hand on your heart and tell yourself these affirmations.

I Am Beautiful
I Am Light
I Love Myself
I Am Love

Anything that gives you affirmation that you are perfect the way you are is good and will help increase your self-worth.

I Am Perfect the Way I Am
I Am Successful
I Am Healthy
I Am Smart
I Am Confident

Alternatively, if you can't remember any of these affirmations, make up your own, or simply state:

I Am Amazing!
I Am Amazing!
I Am Amazing!

Stating affirmations like this can be very helpful to find and accept yourself for who you are. When you state that you are something you want to become, you will become just that. The same is true when you have negative statements about yourself. It is very important that you always think positive thoughts about yourself, as you ultimately create your own reality.

Many people are constantly put down verbally or putting themselves down and after a while may start believing they are not worthy or not beautiful or that they are not smart. Even people who are not put down verbally may not really love themselves. They may be caught up in societal pressures of trying to look like a movie star and may have self-destructive thoughts such as, *I'm too fat; I'm not smart enough,* and compare themselves to others instead of looking inside themselves and accepting and loving themselves for who they are.

You may meet a woman whom you perceive as gorgeous, and she may also have a lot of money. Does this make her happier than you? Of course, it would be easier if you didn't have to worry about your basic needs. However, what we see on the surface is never what is going on underneath. Everyone experience struggles; it doesn't matter what you look like or where you come from. Don't be judgmental. Keep an open mind; maybe the person you are perceiving as having an easy life is struggling to not commit suicide and all they needed from you that day to stay on the earth was a friendly smile and a nice comment. Think before you speak, and be kind to all people; you don't know their struggles.

Stages

When children are young, they go through certain ages, like the terrible twos. Each age group has specific developmental stages as well as behavioral patterns and fears. This goes on through their teen years, and those of you who are parents are familiar with these stages. However, I don't believe these developmental stages stop when you are eighteen or twenty-one. I believe they go on through your whole life. As we become wiser with our life experiences, we look back and remember how we felt at a certain age. It seems like there are certain things we need to do at certain ages and if we don't do them then we do them later, as if there are certain things necessary to experience in order to learn and grow. I feel many women believe they can have it all when they reach their forties. They can be successful at work; look like a teenager; have kids, a husband, or lover; and juggle it all. Sometimes this can backfire as it did for me and make us too obsessive with certain aspects of ourselves. We may go overboard with any or all things in our life such as exercising too much, eating too little, or working too much. Just pushing the envelope too hard in any or all directions instead of creating balance.

Anorexia

When I was young, before I had children, I was a thin, young woman, five foot six and 110 pounds. I could eat anything I wanted without gaining weight. My mother told me that when she was eighteen years old, she would eat whipped cream to try to gain weight. I guess this could be seen as a blessing or curse, depending on how you feel about your body. As I was thin, I naturally wanted to have more curves. I wanted to have bigger breasts and look more voluptuous. All my friends who had curves and bigger breasts naturally wanted to be thin like me and couldn't understand why I wanted to look like them. Many times, I think they thought I was saying that to get attention. It seemed incomprehensible to them that I wanted to be bigger like them. After all, society was telling us that we should be thin as a stick, but I felt that they looked more like a woman and would, therefore, get boyfriends easier. How you perceive things comes from your mind. Watch your thoughts!

When I was in my forties, I felt like I had the chance to reclaim my looks and life—the last chance to look young. It was around 2006, and I was taking the prerequisite classes for med school and felt like I was on top of the world. Somehow, being back in college and having teenagers at home, I became obsessed with looking young and thin. Part of this obsession, I feel, stems from society always hammering us with Photoshopped pictures of women looking skinny, gorgeous, and unnaturally proportioned. This is what many of us aim to look like. I became obsessed with losing weight, and all I wanted was to look the way I had when I was young. First of all, wanting to weigh the same as you weighed in high school or before having children isn't a good idea. I was an adult and had more body fat and bigger breasts. My hormones had also changed to accommodate my adult body. If you are in a position of wanting to lose weight, work with a nutritionist or doctor who can help guide you through a healthy weight loss program.

I started walking up and down the hills in San Francisco and would average sixteen miles per week. Granted, I got in good shape and could easily sprint up those steep hills as my muscle tone improved. I was shrinking one size down at a time. I started out as a size twelve to fourteen, then size ten, size eight, and so on until I was a size zero or two! Yup! That is just crazy for someone in her forties! I was aiming for 110 pounds, as that is what I weighed in high school. Who does that? That is crazy! If you are one of these women, stop right now. We have grown and matured. We need the extra fat. Your body has changed. You typically don't look good at the same weight you were in high school either.

I was obsessed with losing weight, and I wasn't putting enough calories back into my body each day after all that walking. After several months, I had reached 110 pounds. My high school weight. I was a size zero or two, depending on manufacturers, and would always purchase the brand that I was the smallest size in. This is not healthy. You shouldn't care about your clothing size. If someone asks about your size, don't answer the question. It's really none of their business! First of all, manufacturers vary, so your size most likely vary depending on who makes the clothing. If you have Scandinavian genes and are tall according to American standards, you may be a size small in Scandinavia, but if you purchase clothes from Asia, where people are typically of a shorter and smaller build, you may be a size extra large. So, size doesn't matter when it comes to clothing. Don't obsess over it!

As wrong as it was, I was on a mission. I thought if I ate a teaspoon of whipped cream, I would gain weight.

One day, as I arrived at the ballet school in the city to drop off the kids and go for a hike up and down the hills, the mother of one of my son's friends pulled me aside. She said, "We are worried about you. You have lost too much weight." The good news was that I listened. I heard her. I'm very thankful for her brave actions to pull me aside, as I realized that my problem was much bigger than I thought. I went to my walking buddies and told them I would be happy to walk with them, but I needed to make a stop at Whole Foods on the way to purchase some ice cream. I needed to turn this process and unhealthy thinking around. I chose to eat ice cream only because that was one of the hardest things to allow myself to eat, and I figured if I was to tackle my habits, I had to go all out.

I then saw my doctor, who told me that if I lost one more pound, he would put me in the hospital. I laugh at this threat now when looking back, as he knew I was petrified of hospitals after my experience and I would do anything to not have to go there. Smart man! He knew what to say to make me understand I needed to make a change.

I now understood that I had a problem and was forcing myself to eat as much food as the other family members put on their plates. It was difficult, but I knew I had to learn to control my thoughts. My body needed calories to stay healthy. Within a few weeks, I started gaining my weight back, and ever since this event, I have been very aware of eating disorders and how easy it is to get pulled into this type of thinking process. Maybe this also helped me to become a better physician and healer and to help my patients understand their problems better. Eating disorders are rampant in our society, and it is easy to get sucked into this phenomenon even if you think this will never happen to you. I didn't really see it coming, but every time I looked in the mirror, I was obsessed with looking thinner and, as I thought, more beautiful. If I weighed 120 pounds, I would look in the mirror and tell myself I would be more beautiful if I were 115 pounds. When 115 pounds, I would tell myself it would be better if I were 110 pounds, and so on. It is a disease of control; it felt like everything else was out of my control. Only you control what you eat.

If you see yourself in this story, talk to your doctor and get on a good program to recovery and good health. You are beautiful just the way you are!

If you are someone who thinks you must be thin or have to alter your body in some way to please your partner or significant other, take a second look and ask yourself why. Why do you believe your body isn't perfect the way it was made? Why are you listening to someone else telling you how you should look? Do you love yourself? Ask yourself what it is you are trying to control or why you have an obsession with looking a certain way. Taking a deeper look at your life and what you are happy or unhappy about can give you clues as to why you are obsessing over your looks. When we shed our outer appearance and take off our clothes, we are all the same and come in all different sizes and colors, none of which matters. What matters is your beauty within. Be true to yourself. You are love. You are light. You are beautiful.

Diets

As a physician, I often have patients coming in stating their spouse, sister, or friend are telling them to eat a certain diet. Typically, the person telling them is on some diet and is convinced that their spouse or friend would be better off following the same regime. My advice is always to listen to your own body. What works for one person may be a disaster for someone else. Some people do better with grains, while others can have no grains. Some patients need to eat meat, fish, and fowl, while another may be better off being a vegetarian. Some patients experience indigestion with certain foods while another does well on the same foods. Your digestion and wellbeing depend on many different factors. There are so many different issues that can cause similar digestive symptoms, so it's always best to work with a doctor to help you figure out the problem. The moral of this story is, don't listen to other people telling you what to eat or not eat. Listen to your own body and what it is telling you to eat and how you feel after eating those foods.

Self-Love

Self-love is more important than you might think. When I was around twelve years old and becoming more self-conscious about how I looked, I had a terrible complex about my left ear. It would always manage to stick out between my strands of hair, and I thought it looked stupid. I would try to tape my ear to keep it covered by my hair. I asked my dad if I could please have surgery to make my ears match. My dad wasn't too keen on having any kind of medical procedure done that wasn't absolutely necessary, as there are always risks involved.

My mom would tell me I was beautiful the way I was, that God had made me this way and I should be proud and like my body the way it was. Though these words were all well-meaning, I still had a complex. At this age, I would never allow my hair to be cut short, as it would expose my left ear. It wasn't until just a few years ago that I finally became comfortable with a short haircut above my ears. It basically took a big part of my life to get over my not-so-perfect ear. How silly.

If you have something you don't like about yourself, tell yourself that this is unique to you! You are beautiful with this one feature, and nobody else has your body or your special trait. You are perfectly made the way you are!

"The Carousel"

Life, it's like a carousel that never stops,
spinning in a circle until your time is up.

Life, it is everywhere.
Life, the privilege given to us.
Life, our way to exist.
Life, it is what we do.

The carousel, it sometimes makes me dizzy,
dizzy, because it spins too fast.
My surroundings, they pass before my eyes too quickly,
making me unable to grasp an accurate picture of its existence.

I jump off the turning platform to catch my breath.
I notice the carousel is still going;
it didn't stop its rotation because I jumped off.

While I'm off the carousel, I view my world in slow motion.
I notice the deep blue color of the sky.
I notice the lush green color of the grass.
The trees, every leaf so perfectly made,
every pine needle, there for a reason,
all of nature, so perfectly created.

Like a giant greenhouse,
we live in it,
all we need to survive,
all we need to exist,
it is all here,
all here on earth.

I walk among the people on the city streets,
The people, so serious,
looking straight ahead, as if they had blinders
enabling them to only look straight ahead.
They can only see the track ahead of them,
staring, they follow the railroad track,
unable to see their surroundings.

They move in herds, like drones,
some going up the street,
some going down the street,
no eye contact,
you don't know who they are.
Suspicion lurks in the air;
can we trust them?
Is that a good guy or a bad guy?
The people, they seem so lonely,
isolated, longing for contact.

Nobody is laughing,
nobody is smiling.
Isolated, they walk alone,
all strangers to one another.

Embrace one another,
see the humor in what you do,
see the humor in what you say.

Forget about the rat race,
forget about the college,
listen to your heart,
live your life according to your heart,
you merely have to exist.

Take a moment in your life to make the day special for
someone else.
Take a moment to say something nice.
Take a moment to notice your surroundings.

The carousel, it's still going.
It didn't stop because I jumped off.
I run and jump back on to the eternally spinning carousel.

ACV

MESSAGE | Your body is a temple; take good care of it!

Exercise: Think about how you treat your body. Do you take good care of it? Do you take better care of other people or animals than yourself? Take time to rest and reflect. Take time to pamper yourself. Think about what you feed your body. Is the food you eat good fuel for your body? Tell yourself nice things. Be kind to your body, and treat it as a temple.

16

THE SPIRIT WORLD

First Year Out of Medical School
I received my license to practice medicine in October of 2016, and I had already enrolled with the Upledger Institute to study craniosacral therapy and emotional release technique. It was during this fall that I met the friend who gave me the messages from my mother in the spirit world who told me to go to Arthur Findlay College to study mediumship. Time was flying by, and I was busy learning the ropes of practicing medicine full time as well furthering my education.

England
Before I knew it, March 2017 arrived, and I was eager to visit England to learn about the spirit world. I really had no idea what to expect. I still doubted that you could prove that messages from the spirit world were from a specific person. I could understand receiving messages, but how could you call in spirits for someone else and then communicate with them? It seemed a little far-fetched for my left brain to comprehend.

My flight was scheduled for March 29 with arrival in England March 30. I then had one day to rest before classes began on Saturday, April 1. I spent a day at a small country inn about two hours north of London and about fifteen minutes away from the college where I would attend the seminar for the week. As

I was jet-lagged and tired, I decided to watch Netflix and spent six hours watching a brain game show. I was worried I would develop dementia and Alzheimer's in my old age like my mother had, so figured I needed to keep my brain active and stimulated now that I was out of med school.

Saturday finally arrived, and I ordered a taxi to take me from the country inn to the college. I checked in to my dorm room around 3:00 p.m. and had a lovely British woman as my roommate. At 4:30 p.m., I went to the sanctuary where we gathered to learn the details about the program and receive the schedule for the week. I was so excited to find out what was in store for the week.

Even though I had left my body more than once and already understood that the soul survives death, I still needed confirmation that communication with the spirit world was possible. Why was I so skeptical? How many times did I need proof? How could I see events before they happen? How can you get messages from a spirit? How does it all work? My mind was in overdrive trying to figure out the answers to all my questions. After the gathering, we were divided into six groups with about twelve people in each, which were mostly based on our psychic and mediumistic abilities. I joined my newfound friends and headed to dinner in the cafeteria before we would again gather to get signed up for the various events during the week.

As the day came to a close, I headed back to my room. Even though I was tired, I wasn't able to go to sleep, as I was too excited about being at the college and what I would learn the next day. I noticed that my roommate was still awake, so we started talking. It was her first time at the college as well, and we were both bursting at the seams with excitement. I literally felt like a kid in a girls' dorm as we were giggling and whispering to not wake our classmates next door. I felt so alive and so excited!

It had been a long couple of years with a heavy workload, and this was a welcomed change.

When was the last time you did something for yourself that made you feel this way? If you can't even remember or it was a long time ago, think about doing something fun! Find that spark within you!

Communication

The week flew by, and I learned that different people typically communicate in different ways with spirits. Some receive information through auditory channels, clairaudient, while others may receive information through images, clairvoyant, and still others through feelings, clairsentient, or a mixture of all three. The spirits also learn how to communicate with you based on how you receive information. I believe we all have intuitive and psychic abilities. You can probably recall a time when you heard, saw, or felt something and you just knew it was right. Maybe you have been visited by a loved one who has passed on to the spirit world but weren't sure if it was something you really experienced or just made up in your mind. We have mostly forgotten to use these senses, and as we often can't prove why we feel a certain way, we tend to suppress it. Don't suppress these feelings, images, or voices. Listen to them! Maybe someone is trying to give you some guidance.

As the week went on and I learned how to communicate with the spirit world, I was amazed at how someone from anywhere in the world could sit across from me and tell me specific details about the spirit they were communicating with. *You couldn't make these things up even if you tried*, I thought, as the information relayed was very specific to the spirit. The same was true for myself, as I was able to bring messages and specific information to the person I was working with. It was a true eye-opener that our existence here on earth is much more divine than we realize. I finally felt like there was proof that the soul survives the death of the body. I couldn't believe it had taken me a quarter of a century to believe this was true, even though I had left my body myself. How are other people supposed to understand how divine our existence is without having had the experiences in life that I had? I started to understand why the spirit world had asked me to write about the journey of my soul; it was so I could enable other people to develop their intuition and heal their hearts.

My Father-in-Law in Spirit

One evening, my group was the audience for the more advanced students who would work as mediums and place spirits with the audience. As a middle-aged man took to the platform, he told the group that he had an older gentleman with him. As he described the spirit who he was communicating with, I immediately recognized it to be my father-in-law. I raised my hand to show I recognized the spirit he was describing. We were only allowed to say yes or no when he asked if we understood the message and descriptions. We were not allowed to give him any other information. At one point during his reading, he made the gesture of removing his wedding ring. He asked if I understood this gesture. I answered yes. He then told me that they understood why this divorce had taken place and that the spirit world was okay with our decision. My divorce had finalized two weeks before the trip. I felt so relieved, as I wasn't sure if the message was going to be the opposite. I thought he was going to tell me we had made a mistake. It had been a long two years of contemplating if we had made the right decision. It was a great relief to hear the spirit world understood, and it made it easier to deal with the separation, as it felt like this was the way it was supposed to be, at least for now. There were several evidential messages during the reading, and all of them were correct. My mind felt like it was ready to explode from sheer excitement!

My Mother in Spirit

Another day, I had a reading with my teacher, and my mother came through and communicated with her. The medium said, "Your mother is telling me that you started writing a book and that you are to write two books—no, wait, three!" This was the exact same message about writing books that I had been given in 2004 in my living room and then again by my new friend in the fall six months earlier. *Wow, incredible!* I thought. I started laughing, and my jaw dropped as she continued the reading. She was even using expressions that only my mother would use. My mother always used to joke with me as a child and say that when you die you "sit around on a cloud." When she was communicating with my mother, she said my mother was telling her that "she is not just sitting around on a cloud; she is busy doing many things and learning music." She then proceeded to say, "Your mother tells me you don't need to watch all those brain game shows. You're not going to get dementia in old age like she did; you are going to die from something else." I couldn't believe what I'd heard. She knew I had been in the hotel room a few days earlier watching all those brain game shows!

How much of our life is predetermined? Had I in a sense signed up for my life with some give and take for various outcomes and options along the way? It made me realize how divine our existence really is and that the spirit world is always around us. They help us along even if we don't realize or know it. They support us in our earthly lives. I felt light as a feather walking out of my reading. It was true that we could have communication with the spirit world on demand. It would have been impossible for her to know such detailed information about me as well as the fact that I was writing a book and then to deliver the message the exact same way I had received it in 2004. It is all divine, and so are you!

If you have lost a loved one, listen to your messages and open your heart. Maybe they are trying to send you a message showing you they are okay.

The Books

As the last day approached, I was looking in the bookstore at the college and was hoping to find a book I could read on the long eleven-hour flight back to the United States. I scanned all the books and kept coming back to a book on power animals. *Power animals? I don't really know much about that,* I thought. However, I felt like the spirits were nudging me, and I decided to listen to my heart and purchased the book.

After reading the book, I started to pay attention to the animals right outside my house. They would often stop and stare at me, and I would look them up in the book to understand their meaning. I was always amazed at the message the specific animal had in the book. It was always very fitting to what I was experiencing in my life. I wondered if it could be that they were bringing me a message, or was I just looking for and wanting messages? I started to become more aware of everything that was around me. I believe we miss many clues about our world, as we have moved further and further away from our ancient ancestors' knowledge about nature, animals, and the Divine Feminine. Pay attention to your surroundings. Pay attention to what you are doing to Mother Earth. The earth is alive and part of what we are all connected to and through.

Take Time

After a weeklong seminar, I returned home to Arizona and back to work at the clinic. I now understood more than ever that I needed to develop my meditation practice. I had been so busy raising kids, working, and going to medical school, I had forgotten to take care of myself.

We all lead such busy lives and often forget to take time out to just sit still and enjoy our divine existence. Take at least thirty minutes per day for yourself. Sit down and don't look at your computer, phone, or a magazine; simply sit down and sip some tea or water and enjoy the peace and stillness within you. If you live in a city, you can find a bench or park and just watch the birds or people passing by. Take time to just feel yourself in your body. Who are you? Where did you come from? Where are you going? Be grateful for what you have been given in life. There is always something you can be grateful for, even in tough times. Tough times never last forever and help shape us into whom we will become. It will all make sense later.

Bodhi

Before I knew it, August came around. I was lying on my bed in mediation, and I saw an image of a kitten and received the message, *Healing.* The image took me from his face and up to the top of his head. The image was so strong and clear, and I wondered what it meant. The markings on the kitten were very specific, and I thought maybe those markings meant something. What was the meaning of healing? Did the markings mean healing? Or did it mean healing the kitten? Or maybe the kitten had healing abilities?

I lay in bed for ten minutes contemplating the meaning of the message. As I wasn't able to connect the dots, I put it at the back of my mind and figured it would eventually make sense.

About four weeks later, I decided to get a kitten. It was time to bring some new life into the house, and I had missed not having any animals for the past year and a half. I looked online at the listings and saw two kittens that looked cute. I met the mother and her daughter at the grocery store and decided to adopt the little six-week-old male kitten that had black stripes on his gray fur. I named him Bodhi.

I returned home and gave him the food they had told me he would eat. It was now evening, and he didn't want to eat anything. I figured he would probably eat after he felt more at home and went to sleep. The next morning, it didn't look like he had touched his food. I immediately went to the pet store to get some wet food and formula. Nothing seemed to work, and as I was lying on the floor looking straight at his little face, I noticed that his markings were the exact same ones I had seen in the meditation. Instantaneously, I knew the message from the meditation meant I had to heal the kitten! I shoved down a sandwich and took off to the vet. It turned out he had congestion in his chest. As he was so tiny, the vet said he had a 50/50 chance of survival. I was given clear instructions on how to give him his medications and to feed him Karo syrup. I had to wake him up every two hours and then have him lick baby food off my fingers. He recovered quickly and was soon licking baby food himself from a tiny bowl. He was most likely just weaned too quickly, so I let the mother know what happened so she could help protect the other kittens.

How often do we receive messages and then discount them? Can you think of times you have received a message and then not remembered them until they materialized? Listen to your inner Divine Feminine, and let that intuitive power come to the surface.

Priyala

I now had a kitten but still longed for a dog. I really missed not having animals around me, especially as I was living on my own for the first time in my life. I had been looking at the online listings for months in search of a labradoodle but hadn't been able to find one. In December, when my sister-in-law was visiting, I saw a listing with puppies a two-hour drive from where I lived. I told my sister-in-law, and of course, she encouraged me to go take a look at the puppies. This was the daughter of my mother-in-law who had always encouraged me to "just get it."

I instantly fell in love with the black female in the litter. There was a special bond between us right from the start, as she kept coming back to me. Within an hour, we were back in the car, with my sister-in-law holding the little puppy in her lap as I started the drive back home. For me, animals help me stay grounded. They help me de-stress. They make me go outside and enjoy life. They make me realize that the things I think are important really aren't! If you own a pet, give it a hug!

Second Trip to England

I was busy working and caring for my kitten and puppy, and a year had already passed. I had written more than half of this book, and it was now March 2018. It was time to return to England and Arthur Findlay College to develop my mediumship skills.

During my first visit to the college a year earlier, I had been touched deeply by the messages that came through when working with the students and teachers. It allowed me to understand how close we are to the spirit world. As we are wired for survival, most of us tend to go through life not thinking about the fact that we will all die someday, but death is really just a continuation of our soul's journey without our current body.

As I understand it, you can't really call in a specific spirit.

The spirit world decides who is to come through to deliver a message to you. It makes sense, as you may not be ready to hear from certain spirits if you didn't have a good relationship with them while they were on earth or perhaps the message would have a stronger impact on you if it came from a certain spirit. They are very intelligent and often come through to apologize for the harm they caused you during their life. They are very aware of what we do and how we feel at all times.

On the first day of class, my teacher came close to me, and he gave me a message that I had a story to tell. He looked at me and said, "The story is about your life, and it will help other people heal as they read about your journey." I was stunned. Since I had started writing my book, I had wished it would bring health, hope, and healing to those who would read it. I was so excited and trusted that he was right.

Time after time, I would receive very specific messages like this. As I pondered the significance of these messages, it suddenly dawned on me what the meaning of the message was that I had received in the living room in 2004 about bringing "messages and healing" to the people. The "message" I was to bring was how we referred to the "messages" we receive from the spirit world. I now understood why I had been sent to Arthur Findlay College to develop my mediumistic abilities. I was to bring "messages" from the spirit world to the people to help them heal. It all finally made sense. Of course, they had told me in 2004 that I would understand what they meant later, but I didn't know anything about mediumship back then, and I had to keep traveling on my road until one day it would make sense. I also understood what the spirit guide had meant by dividing my time between working as a physician and other work. I was so happy to solve this last puzzle piece after fourteen years of wondering what the meaning was.

Life is a journey, and sometimes we don't understand why we are doing what we are doing or where our road is taking us, but it will eventually bring clarity and peace to our soul's purpose.

MESSAGE | Find the peace within you, and you will experience the connection to all that is.

Exercise: Take time out each day to sit quietly for thirty minutes to an hour. You can play relaxing meditation music or sit in the quiet. After you have been sitting quietly every day for a few months, you will start to notice how peaceful you are becoming when sitting still. It is a time of inward reflection as well as connecting with our divine existence on earth and the universe. You may start to have spiritual experiences, and your clairvoyance, intuition, and insight may become more refined. To advance in your own healing and understanding of your divine existence requires that you be still in meditation on a regular basis. It is through the stillness that you become more advanced in your spiritual abilities, for it is through the stillness that you become one with all that is.

17

HEALING THE
DIVINE FEMININE

Yin and Yang

Each person has what we call yin, a feminine quality, and yang, a masculine quality, which creates a balance between the two. Everything has a yin and yang aspect. Animals and plants and even the planets in our solar system are assigned feminine or masculine qualities. The feminine energy, or yin, is on our left side of the body, and yang energy, the masculine energy, is on our right side. The yin and yang that exists within all of us is connected through energetic channels, a life force. There is a delicate balance within this system with a sort of give and take environment to balance the energies. You don't want to have too much yang or too little yin or vice versa, as you would not be in balance. It is the same with all that exists. When we create too much of one energy, it causes our lives, health, and the world to become unbalanced.

We refer to earth as Mother Earth and the moon as female. We refer to the sun as male. Even though we assign feminine or masculine qualities to objects, they still have the essence of both female and male. The yin or feminine energy is the dark part of the yin/yang symbol and connects with your womb as well as Mother Earth. It is the receiving energy. The yang, the masculine energy, is the more penetrative and forceful energy, such as taking charge or making decisions kind of energy and is the light part of the yin/yang symbol. However, men also have yin energy, female energy, even though they don't have a uterus, and women, of course, have yang energy. We call this duality. We exist in a dualistic world where everything has an opposite, or at least that is how we perceive it. If we didn't have an opposite to everything, there would be nothing to balance, and our souls would therefore not progress and learn. If we only experienced happiness, we wouldn't understand sadness. We need an opposite to understand the world around us.

Energy

You have most likely felt energy from other people, and some people can easily feel how other people are feeling, and we refer to them as empaths. Have you ever walked into a room and known that there was anger and frustration present either from one person toward you or between other people in the room? You can most likely feel the anger in the air, and you know without speaking that there is a problem. The same goes true for love. You can most likely feel if someone has feelings for you without the person telling you. This is all energy, and you create energy with your thoughts and actions. We are like little energetic bundles that hold, generate, give, and receive energy.

Think about how we perform an EKG on the heart. We measure electricity. According to polarity studies, the right side of your body is positive, and the left side is negative. The upper part of your body is positive and the lower part negative. The front side is positive, and the backside is negative. As you can see, you are full of electricity. A magnet also has positive and negative poles, and if you've ever played with magnets, you know that the positive and negative poles attract each other. It works the same way in your body. All those negative and positive charges in your body attract each other and make things flow. When you are out of balance, you will not feel well. The energy that flows through your body is referred to as chi, ki, prana, or life force, to mention a few names. If you think of acupuncture meridians, they are channels of energy currents through your body. It's already been proven that your body doesn't just react through chemical reactions but also through electrical signals called piezoelectricity. We are literally charged with electricity.

The earth gives off negative ions that we absorb through our feet when walking barefoot on the earth, which is referred to as grounding. We are dependent on the balance of all that is, including the energy coming from Mother Earth and outer space.

Energy is everywhere. Some energy we can measure and feel while others may come through spiritual forces. The law of conservation states, "Energy is never created nor destroyed." Energy is recycled repeatedly. Recycle your negative energy out to the universe, and replace it with positive, happy energy. When you have negative thoughts, stop for a moment and say in your mind or out loud, "I'm letting go of [insert what you are letting go of], and I send this energy out to the universe to be recycled. I'm replacing this energy with love and gratitude."

Everyone is a bundle of spiritual energy. Think of your cell phone; can you see the Wi-Fi signal? Most likely not. But your phone receives and sends signals as well as interprets them. You are the same as a cell phone in this respect. You also send and receive signals. Some signals that you can easily identify are typically those of anger and love. What signals are you sending out? Are your signals negative or positive? Do you see the glass as half full or half empty? Are you happy in your heart? Think about the signals you send out; others can feel them.

I believe there is an intricate energetic balance between

everything that exists. Every leaf, rock, and molecule are connected and affected by every action and thought of everything and everyone that exists. I'm sure you can relate to this, as we can see how the world around us is affected by the extinction of animals. One animal feeds another. If one animal dies out, the animals that fed on that animal may die out, too. We are all connected, and if you disturb the existence of one species, you disturb the whole food chain, which in turn affects everything else. All are connected to the grid and, therefore, depend on one another. There is a delicate balance between all that is, and it's our responsibility to maintain it.

Healing

You create your life through your own belief system. Of course, some of the things we experience are part of our journey to learn and grow. It doesn't matter how much we don't want to be sick or in a sticky situation, as it may just be part of our journey. However, try to always look at things from a positive perspective. Don't forget to laugh, and don't forget that whatever situation you are in, nothing lasts forever. If you are having difficulties in life, imagine your heart is already healed. See your heart as even stronger than it was before you started experiencing difficulties. You have to heal yourself and your problems in life in order to help heal others and stay on your chosen path. Stay true to yourself.

What bothers you in life? Do you feel controlled, manipulated, suffocated, or submissive? Can you change it? Surround yourself and your soul with beautiful colors that you create in your mind. Your mind has a tremendous capacity to overcome obstacles if you allow it to help you. Take the time to nurture your own body, mind, and spirit. There is only one of you, and you are unique to this world. Embrace and empower yourself!

Backpack

We are all given obstacles in life to overcome. Sometimes you may look at a friend or neighbor thinking, *Boy, she has such an easy life. She doesn't have to worry about having enough money to feed her family.* However, many times, these people have other struggles that you may not be aware of. They may be struggling with addictions such as alcohol and drugs, or they may have children with addictions and worry about them. They may be battling a disease you are not aware of.

I often feel like all people have been given a backpack full of troubles at birth that we carry around with us throughout life. The amount of troubles in our backpack depends on what we signed up for in this life. Ultimately, I believe we are here to evolve our soul, and the weight of our backpack is a measure of what we need to resolve and learn in this lifetime. You may say that your life has been full of abuse and disease. Turn the table around and say, "I signed up for a lot in this life! I'm going to resolve all my issues, past and present, in this life, and my soul will grow tremendously." By shifting your perception, you will gain a different perspective.

I agree it doesn't seem fair that some have to suffer more than others. However, all we can do is focus on healing ourselves in order to become whole. The next time you feel like you are struggling with too many obstacles in your life, remember that you are unloading troubles from your backpack that you signed up for at birth. As soon as you start to unload and resolve your problems, the load will be lighter. It may take years to resolve issues or it may only take a few moments, depending on the complexity of it all. Many times, you have to dig down deep into your soul to figure out why things are the way they are. Other times, you may not understand why you had to go through something until later in life when you realize that the person you have become resulted from your life experiences, as difficult as they may have been at the time. Sometimes it takes time until we understand that those experiences have shaped us to become the person we are today. It takes a lot of self-work and understanding to resolve issues and move forward.

Perception - WWMHS

We all live our lives from our own perception. How you interpret everyday experiences is based on your perception. You may be joking with a friend, but they might not think the joke is funny, as it may be related to a bad memory. We all interpret things we see, hear, or feel differently based on our own perception and life experiences.

When you deal with other people, are you judging and basing your interpretations on what feels good for your own ego? Let go of your ego and try to focus your view and perception from your heart, not your mind. Ask yourself, What would my heart say? (WWMHS)

Shaman Itzhak Beery stated during the interview *Shamanic Healing with Itzhak Beery* on July 10, 2019, by EntheoRadio, that there is an old prophecy by the Inca which began around 1993, which states that the eagle of the north and the condor of the south will fly together in harmony. This will signify the return of the feminine energy and the leadership of the heart instead of the mind. It will create a balance between the heart and the mind. The eagle symbolizes the mind, whereas the condor symbolizes the heart and intuition. We are now, according to the prophecy, in that potential window where we have the opportunity to raise our consciousness and connect our heart and mind.

Let Go

Let go of seeking approval from others, and focus on who you are and what the best option is for your life. You don't need approval from others to follow your heart. Let go of old patterns and thoughts. Write letters of forgiveness to people who are alive or in spirit. How would you live your life if you were told you only had six months left to live? Would it change how you treat other people? Would it change what you are grateful for? Live your life every day as if you only had six months left.

We are all responsible for our actions and thoughts. Make your thoughts worthwhile. Set intentions every day of who you are and what you want to become. Set intentions for being kinder, being stronger, healthier, or whatever you want to create in your life.

Trust in Your Messages

We all receive messages from higher divine forces, whether we recognize them or not. In 2004, when I received the messages from the spirit guide to go to medical school, to combine East and West, to bring messages to people and write three books, I wasn't sure how significant they were to my life path. However, I listened. I had to trust the message.

Whatever stage you are at in your life, listen to your calling from deep inside your soul. Always remember that you are on your own unique special path in life. You are fine just where you are.

Frequencies

In Dr. John Beaulieu's book *Human Tuning Sound Healing with Tuning Forks* published by BioSonic Enterprises, he states, "The Perfect Fifth, C and G, is the interval of ideal nervous system tuning. The Perfect Fifth bring all parts of our self into a unified harmony." When using two tuning forks such as C and G, the two notes from the tuning forks merge and create a third sound. Dr. Beaulieu says, "The third sound is called a different tone in a musical language because it is simply the difference in frequency between the two tuning forks. The Pythagoreans, based on their experience, called the difference tone the 'voice of God.'"

The physical Universe is an aggregate of frequencies.
—Buckminster Fuller

Resonance
Dr. John Beaulieu continues and describes resonance as follows: "Resonance comes from the Latin verb *resonare*, meaning to 'return to sound.' It means to sound and resound as in an echo." He continues by describing different types of resonance such as sympathetic resonance, which happens when one tuning fork tuned to a specific frequency is struck, causing another tuning fork of the same frequency to also vibrate at the same tone even though it was not touched. "Resonance can be understood as a merging created when energy moves back and forth between two or more bodies." Dr. Beaulieu then describes cognitive resonance, which takes place when someone talks about a concept that we agree with and how politicians often use this tactic to gain voters. He then continues by talking about faith healers: "They lay their hands on the body and allow themselves to empathetically resonate wherever spirit leads them. The resulting interaction between the person and healer becomes a divine communion. A resonate 'returning to sound' creates a healing response."

Think about the energy you create and send out to the world. Are you creating resonance or dissonance with your thoughts and actions?

Synchronization and Entrainment
In the book *The Secret Teachings of Plants: The Intelligence of the Heart in the Direct Perception of Nature* by Stephen Harrod Buhner, he talks about the electromagnetic field around the heart

and how it synchronizes and entrains with other electromagnetic fields that it comes in contact with. Our heart, therefore, has the ability to affect other organisms.

When you move your focus to the heart on gratitude and love, you are changing the energy inside of you as well as the energy you project out. The frequency that you create inside of you is, therefore, the frequency you send out and look to resonate with. If you send out bad vibes, you are essentially attracting bad vibes. If you send out good vibes, you attract good vibes. Pay attention to your thought pattern, for you create and attract what you create in your mind.

In Bruce H. Lipton's book, *The Honeymoon Effect: The Science of Creating Heaven on Earth,* he describes the effect the environment has on our cells. During one of his experiments, he learned that cells in a petri dish grew different kinds of cells—bone, muscle, or fat—depending on the environment the cells were in. The environment we create internally in our bodies is therefore of utmost importance in order to create a happy and healthy life.

Light

As you have traveled with me on my journey through this book, I hope you have let light into your own heart. Think of this light as a burning candle that increases in intensity as you allow yourself to listen to your heart. This light can illuminate the whole world. By your light shining brighter, you help others increase the intensity of their lights, which in turn helps illuminate and heal the world. From my out-of-body experiences, it is my understanding that we come from light and return to light. We are light.

Your heart has the ability to feel love both in physical and spiritual form. The heart is what you should focus the attention on, not your mind. It is your heart that feels when something is right or wrong. Listen to it.

Yesterday I was clever, so I wanted to change the world.
Today I am wise, so I am changing myself.
— Rumi

The Hourglass

I created "The Hourglass" below to help you develop your trust and find your soul's purpose. The title is to remind you that there is no time in the spirit world. I see time as a paradox, as to me, it only exists on the earth-plane and is how we perceive things. "The Hourglass" reminds us that life is eternal. You can keep turning the hourglass around over and over again, and the sand will continue to drop from the upper level to the lower level. Just like the sand flows from both ends, so does the poem. It doesn't matter from which end the sand flows. The result will be the same each time. It is like the circle of life. Eternal. Start by sitting quietly as long as time permits and fill your body with light and extend it out to the universe. Read the poem and allow yourself to experience the meaning of the words.

"The Hourglass"

I trust the inner knowledge I carry in my soul and heart.
I take a deep breath and fill my body with white light.
I shine my bright light from my soul and heart.
I extend my light into the world and sky.
I am the person I want to be.
I listen to my messages.
I am connected.
I am divine.
I am light.
I am love.
I am.

I am.
I am love.
I am light.
I am divine.
I am connected.
I listen to my messages.
I am the person I want to be.
I extend my light into the world and sky.
I shine my bright light from my soul and heart.
I take a deep breath and fill my body with white light.
I trust the inner knowledge I carry in my soul and heart.

Divine Feminine

The Divine Feminine energy is the intuitive, creative, nurturing, and loving balance of all that is. It is what we are all created from and part of. It is the connection of our own heart and soul to Mother Earth and creation. It is the mother of all energy. Without the Divine Feminine, you would not exist, as you were created and born from it. It is this sacred piece of information we have forgotten. We look at our world, trees, plants, people, and the earth in a materialistic way, forgetting that it is all sacred. We are all connected to it and through it. We exist and depend on it.

The Divine Feminine has nothing to do with how you identify sexually. The Divine Feminine is the nurturing and loving energy that surrounds us and exists within all of us, male and female. When you nurture the Divine Feminine, you no longer need to compete or satisfy your ego. You just are. You recognize that all is love and comes from love. You connect your heart with your mind, not your mind with your heart, allowing your heart to become your guide.

The Divine Feminine force is suppressed in our society as well as globally. Our nations and populations are too involved in competing for power and economic strength. We have forgotten what Divine Feminine means. We have forgotten where we came from.

What has happened? Why or when did we lose our respect for the Feminine? How do we heal? In order to create peace, health, and happiness, we need to recognize and nurture the Divine Feminine that exists within all of us. We need to heal the Divine Feminine within ourselves in order to heal the world.

Love begins with loving oneself unconditionally. By finding your own path and happiness in life, you create peace and heal the Divine Feminine within you. As we are all connected, healing yourself will help to heal the whole. When we find peace and happiness within our soul and heart, we affect other people in a positive way. Stay true to yourself and your passion in life.

By sharing my story—the good and the bad, the funny and the sad—I hope it has brought you health, hope, and healing. I hope it has touched your heart and inspired you to develop your own inner wisdom and talents. Don't allow yourself to be suppressed by society and the people around you. Listen to your soul.

Follow your own path and inner guidance in life to create your own journey and happiness in this lifetime. By healing and empowering yourself, you will help heal the world as well as all its inhabitants. You will help heal the Divine Feminine that exists within all of us. We are all connected. We are all one. It is all divine and so are you.

MESSAGE | By healing the Divine Feminine within yourself, you help heal the world.
We are all connected.
We are all one.
It is all divine, and so are you.

Exercise: Whenever you are contemplating how to respond to something or what to do next, move your thought to your heart, and ask your heart what the answer to your question is. WWMHS?

MESSAGES AND EXERCISES

Chapter 1

MESSAGE | Live each day as if it is your last.
Exercise: Remind yourself how precious life is and that anything can happen to you at any given time that may change your life forever. Take the opportunities to enjoy your life whenever you can. This can be something as simple as going to the movies with a friend or enjoying a nice dinner. Keep a daily log, and write down each day one or more events or things you did that made the day special. Did you give a nice compliment to someone, or did someone give you a compliment that changed your day? Did you help an elderly person cross the street or hold the door open for someone that returned your favor with a smile? Small acts of kindness can change both yours and the recipient's life. Find something you can enjoy each day to bring love and gratitude for your life to the present moment.

Chapter 2

MSSAGE | Watch your thoughts; you create what you think. Use your thoughts to create the outcome that you want.
Exercise: Write down what you want to create in your life. Tape this paper to your desk, fridge, mirror, or anywhere you will see it several times per day. If you would like to become a successful salesperson, then visualize yourself as already being this person. If you want to become a better runner, visualize yourself as the best runner you can think of. Create in your mind that you are already the person you are trying to become. Practice this every day.

Chapter 3

MESSAGE | Always focus on gratitude.

Exercise: Make a list every day and write down five things you are grateful for. This is a good exercise that will help you see the positive things in your life that we otherwise tend to take for granted. You have to write down new things you are grateful for each day, and after a while you will see even the smallest things bring you gratitude.

Chapter 4

MESSAGE | Your existence is divine.

Exercise: Have you had spiritual experiences? If so, have you shared them with someone you can trust? As we are spiritual, intuitive creatures, most of us have had intuitive moments. Notice when you have a gut feeling about something and trust it. To develop your intuitive senses, pay attention to how you feel and to what your intuition is telling you at all times. It could be something silly like knowing someone is going to call you and then they call you just when you are about to call them. Write down every time something like this happens, and you will soon discover a pattern of your intuitive abilities. Don't ignore or suppress your intuition, and don't let anyone else influence you to discount them. Embrace your intuitive self.

Chapter 5

MESSAGE | Never ever give up hope.

Exercise: When you feel like you are stuck and hopeless, remember that your experiences in life are transient. Nothing lasts forever. When you feel hopeless, take time to ground yourself. Sit still and just breathe. Notice how many beautiful things you can see around you. Replace your thoughts of hopelessness with gratitude. Do something nice for yourself. It could be taking a bath, journaling, drinking a cup of tea and lighting a candle, drawing, watching a movie, or talking to a friend. Allow yourself to get a little pampered and feel special. There is only one of you, and you are magnificent and special the way you are. Treasure that!

Chapter 6

MESSAGE | Develop your intuitive abilities by acknowledging what you see, hear, or feel.

Exercise: When you have moments of feeling like someone is telling you something or catching a glimpse of something in your mind, tell someone about these moments or write them down in a notebook or on your phone. Keep a list of these intuitive moments so you can go back and verify that you, in fact, did have a premonition about something. When we don't write these moments down or tell someone, we may later question if we really did have knowledge about a future event or if we are experiencing déjà vu. Don't be discouraged if you get some of the information wrong in the beginning; just keep practicing.

Chapter 7

MESSAGE | What is your journey? Listen to your heart and your own inner wisdom! Don't live to please others; live to please yourself.

Exercise: When you wake up in the morning, ask yourself if you are looking forward to your day. When you go to bed at night, are you excited about tomorrow? If not, then ask yourself what makes you want to wake up the next morning. What makes you "tick"? What inside you could you do all day without being bored? What do you do that makes time fly? When you start paying attention to these things, you will start to understand what your natural talent is. It could be something you think is silly and will never support you; however, if you take small steps to allow yourself to do the things you love, they will eventually lead to greater satisfaction and happiness in your life and may someday actually become the way you support yourself.

Chapter 8

MESSAGE | Find happiness in your heart.

Exercise: What makes you happy? Whatever it is that brings happiness to your heart, find time each day to cultivate this. Even if it is only ten minutes a day in the beginning until you rearrange your schedule to include more time for your special activity, the time you set aside will add up. You have to start in order for a change to occur. Once you start, the intention has been set and your life will start to unfold in a different direction.

Chapter 9

MESSAGE | Don't suppress your children's voices. Listen to them. Maybe you were given a particular child in this life to help *you* see the world through a different lens.

Exercise: If you have children of your own or have nieces and nephews or maybe younger siblings, think about how you treat them. Are they telling you things you are uncomfortable with? Are they trying to teach *you* something? Pay attention to the children around you; they may be bringing *you* messages.

Chapter 10

MESSAGE | Just do it!

Exercise: Are you spontaneous? If not, create some spontaneity in your life. Do something you usually wouldn't do. If you never allow yourself to have fun on a work night, then allow yourself to do something fun on these nights to break up the monotony in your life. Just do it!

Chapter 11

MESSAGE | You will never get anywhere in life if you don't take chances. The worst thing that will happen is that you fail and then you'll have to try again. Trust your soul, your messages, and your heart!

Exercise: Take time to be still and close your eyes for fifteen minutes to an hour each day, and you will start to tune in to your guides. They are always around you and willing to help you on your journey. After sitting quietly for about fifteen minutes, ask your spirit guides, using your thoughts, a specific question or sign and see what comes to your mind. Write down the question and answer you get so that later on you can verify it actually happened and it wasn't a figment of your imagination.

Chapter 12

MESSAGE | Never ever give up on your dreams!
Exercise: What are your dreams? Start something that will move you toward your dream. It could be taking a class, painting, writing, playing an instrument, or anything you always wanted to do. Set time aside each day to fulfill your dreams. What makes you "tick"? Who are you? What makes you want to wake up in the morning? Write down all your dreams and then pick the one that your gut tells you to develop. You can also ask your spirit guides for help in making the next move. You have to start in order to create change and fulfill your dreams.

Chapter 13

MESSAGE | The darkness holds the power of creativity and transformation. It is from the darkness that new life awakens and begins.
Exercise: When you feel like you can barely take another day of life and nothing seems to be going in the right direction, remind yourself that this, too, shall pass. Tell yourself that you are strong. Remind yourself that you are sowing your seeds, and soon your flowers will blossom. Send yourself an email with this message or write it down and put it on your mirror or wall to remind yourself daily.

Chapter 14

MESSAGE | It's never too late to make a change and follow your heart.

Exercise: Small steps lead to bigger steps. Take initiative and start the process of working toward your goal. It doesn't matter how old you are. If we live to be one hundred years old and you are fifty right now, you haven't even lived half of your adult life yet. Be brave and take a step toward change, as once you start rolling your snowball, it will gain momentum, and after a while, it will roll by itself.

Chapter 15

MESSAGE | Your body is a temple; take good care of it!

Exercise: Think about how you treat your body. Do you take good care of it? Do you take better care of other people or animals than yourself? Take time to rest and reflect. Take time to pamper yourself. Think about what you feed your body. Is the food you eat good fuel for your body? Tell yourself nice things. Be kind to your body, and treat it as a temple.

Chapter 16

MESSAGE | Find the peace within you, and you will experience the connection to all that is.

Exercise: Take time out each day to sit quietly for thirty minutes to an hour. You can play relaxing meditation music or sit in the quiet. After you have been sitting quietly every day for a few months, you will start to notice how peaceful you are becoming when sitting still. It is a time of inward reflection as well as connecting with our divine existence on earth and the universe. You may start to have spiritual experiences and your clairvoyance, intuition, and insight may become more refined. To advance in your own healing and understanding of your divine existence requires that you be still in meditation on a regular basis. It is through the stillness that you become more advanced in your spiritual abilities, for it is through the stillness that you become one with all that is.

Chapter 17

MESSAGE | By healing the Divine Feminine within yourself, you help heal the world.
We are all connected.
We are all one.
It is all divine, and so are you.
Exercise: Whenever you are contemplating how to respond to something or what to do next, move your thought to your heart and ask your heart what the answer to your question is. WWMHS?

NOTES

I hope you have enjoyed the journey through this book and
that it has allowed you to open your heart to the endless
possibilities that life presents.

Visit www.DrLotte.com and
enter the code below to receive a free meditation.

Code: **Bookpromo**

Made in the USA
Monee, IL
19 January 2022

89253018R00135